D1544210

The Saturnian Quest

John Cowper Powys among the mountains
near Llangollen

The Saturnian Quest

A chart of the prose works of
John Cowper Powys

by G. Wilson Knight

Emeritus Professor of English Literature
in the University of Leeds

NEW YORK

BARNES & NOBLE, INC.

Publishers · Booksellers · Since 1873

First published in 1964
© *G. Wilson Knight, 1964*
Printed in Great Britain by
Villiers Publications Ltd
London NW5

For
PHYLLIS PLAYTER
to whom the gratitude of all who honour
the works of
JOHN COWPER POWYS
must remain
unbounded

Contents

References for *Wolf Solent* and *A Glastonbury Romance* are given to both the two English editions. References and dates for other books, except for *Rodmoor* which has only been published in America, apply to the English editions.

Ah, I must follow it high and low,
Tho' it leave me cold to your human touch !
Some starry sorcery made me so;
And from my birth have I been such.

John Cowper Powys, ' The Saturnian '.

PREFACE

When Mr Derek Langridge asked me to contribute an introductory essay on Powys for his work at present in progress *John Cowper Powys : a Record of Achievement,* I was happy, as well as honoured, in the suggestion. Mr Langridge's volume will contain bibliographical, and a wide range of other, material of first importance to all students of Powys.

This introduction I started in the late summer of 1962, planning a piece of some 6,000 words. Since it was to be a considered and comprehensive statement, I re-read some of the texts; and then, in the manner to which I have grown accustomed, the works under examination started to reveal patterns of which I had not been previously conscious. As had happened to me with Shakespeare in the thirties, so was it now with Powys; what had seemed, though indubitably great, yet nevertheless chaotic, began to disclose patterns that were then recognised as the true source of the 'greatness' already recognised. I decided to re-examine all the books and was soon engaged on an extensive study, which was completed by Christmas, running to some 45,000 words. Despite its length Mr Langridge's publishers, The Scorpion Press, took it on, and it was set up in galleys.

Since a number of considerations, including Mr Powys's death during the summer of 1963, forced the postponement of the main volume, it seemed advisable, in view both of this delay and also of my essay's length, to split off my own contribution and publish it alone. This has been done with the ready concurrence, for which I am deeply grateful, both of Mr Langridge and of Mr John Rolph and Mr Jack Hobbs, directors of the Scorpion Press. I am grateful to Messrs Methuen & Co for undertaking the transfer under such unusual circumstances.

The following pages constitute yet another adventure in what I call ' interpretation '. I have throughout avoided judgments of value, taking each book in turn as a self-subsisting entity with a view to the exploration of its deepest meaning and, as a necessary consequence, an understanding of the relationship of one work to another and to the whole corpus of which each is a limb. This is not quite ' criticism ', as usually understood. For my writing on Powys of a more conventional and indirect, persuasive, discursive or — if I may coin the word —

9

discussive kind, I would point to my various reviews and other essays during recent years.

Among these I would here record the long essay on Powys's general achievement, written on the publication of *Up and Out* for *The Times Literary Supplement* of 11 October, 1957; also my review of *Homer and the Aether* in that journal on 1 May, 1959; and in *The Twentieth Century*, to reviews of *Lucifer* in November, 1956, of Powys's *Letters to Louis Wilkinson* in July, 1958, and of *Homer and the Aether* in May, 1959. *The Yorkshire Post* printed another review of the *Letters* on 15th May, 1958, and commissioned a general article for Powys's ninetieth birthday, published as 'Homage to Powys' on 6 October, 1962. I would also draw attention to my relating of Powys to two famous contemporaries in my article 'Lawrence, Joyce and Powys' in *Essays in Criticism* (Oxford), October, 1961; and to an interesting item, from a psychic angle, in *Psychic News* (London) on 27 July, 1963. There was also my interpretation — which may have done much to set the manner of my interpretations in the following pages — of *Owen Glendower*, contributed to the issue of *A Review of English Literature* (London) which Professor A. N. Jeffares, by a fine stroke of editorial policy, devoted to Powys in January, 1963.

Two broadcasts may be recorded. I was courteously invited by Mr Raymond Garlick to contribute a talk on the novels to a symposium for the Welsh Home Service of the British Broadcasting Corporation, broadcast on 27 June, 1957; and I was myself subsequently honoured by an invitation from Mr Dyfnallt Morgan, of that service, to arrange another grouping of talks in celebration of Mr Powys's ninetieth birthday. In this I was fortunate in obtaining contributions from Mr H. P. Collins, who has himself a study of Powys in hand; Mr Malcolm Elwin, biographer of Llewelyn Powys; Dr George Steiner of Cambridge; and Mr Angus Wilson. A notable poem was composed for the occasion by Mr Francis Berry. The programme, under the production of Mr Morgan, was broadcast on 9 October, 1962.

Though I have for many years been closely involved in Powys's writings — the paragraphs of commentary published in *Christ and Nietzsche* in 1948 were composed before the war — yet it would be an error to regard my present study as no more than a condensation of impressions formulated during those years. The truth is rather different. For, as I have already indicated, under the more deliberated will to a considered and authoritative investigation new and precise patterns unrolled. What seems to happen — I think the matter important enough, and sufficiently misunderstood, to warrant these remarks — is this. One sees suddenly, as from dissolving clouds, a new structure of inner meaning, which might also be called a 'heart' or an 'essence'; it is something which, once seen, is unquestionably there, and which moreover seems to render other effects harmonious by throwing them into new, centripetal, relevance. It also happens that by recognising the true centres of meaning one is enabled to cover a great amount of ground in a comparatively short space. Had I not focussed the 'Saturnian' and 'Cerne Giant' keys to Powys's life-work the substance of the following pages would have been many times more cumbrous and vastly more extended. The result is less a 'critical' discussion, with all the attendant subtleties and reservations characteristic of such writing, than a sharp and defined exposition of the various themes and powers whose interplay makes the literature in question. This is what I call, and it is a phenomenon new in our time, 'interpretation'. True, there may be, and in a pioneer study like this there certainly will be, errors; but they will be errors that can, when discovered, be precisely demonstrated. The margin for individual disagreement, though it exists, is comparatively small, and will be a matter of emphasis, not of fact. My main results, here and elsewhere, are, whether right or wrong, factual. It is accordingly my hope that this map of a hitherto mysterious terrain may prove a clarification and a basis for those many readers for whom Powys has hitherto appeared a great but amorphous genius.

Since Mr Richard Heron Ward's necessarily limited study *The Powys Brothers* in 1935 Britain has produced no attempt at a full-length survey of Powys's achievement. Mr Louis Wilkinson's *Welsh Ambassadors,* published under the pen-name 'Louis Marlow' in 1936, is a mainly personal contribution leading up to the remarkable volume of letters so excellently edited by Mr Wilkinson in 1958. The lack hitherto of any adequate academic and critical attention to so great a writer is strange. On this subject it fell to me, basing my letter on a forceful and timely complaint of Dr George Steiner's in an earlier issue to which my attention had been called by Miss Stella Williams, to start a correspondence in *The Times Literary Supplement* of 17 November, 1961, which elicited some interesting rejoinders, though a peculiarly valuable one from Mr Kewal Motwani was unfortunately too late for publication.

The neglect in question is surely evidence of some serious limitation in our contemporary literary understanding. The nature of this limitation can, as I see it, be quite simply defined. Whereas in every age writers of genius — the very word ' genius ' suggests as much — are saturated in occult perception, the academic and critical intelligence distrusts, in every age, such categories. Now in studying many writers we can avoid direct reference to them, up to a point, by the use of evasive labels such as ' symbolist ', ' impressionism ', ' surrealism ' and so on, without any real fear of commitment. With Powys we cannot do this, if only because he has written so much deliberate propaganda for his own esoteric life-way. This is a ' life-way ' close to the heart and process of creation; and it is noteworthy that much of the interest he has aroused during the last few decades has come from creative artists of different generations and widely differing qualities, such as John Redwood Anderson, J. D. Beresford, Francis Berry, Tom Blackburn, Oliver Campion, Theodore Dreiser, Raymond Garlick, James Hanley, L. P. Hartley, John Heath-Stubbs, Geoffrey Hill, Kenneth Hopkins, Augustus John, Bernard Jones, Laurence Kitchin, Edgar Lee Masters, Huw Menai, Henry Miller, Dimitrije Mitrinovic, Elizabeth Myers, George D. Painter, J. B. Priestley, Edith Sitwell, Stevie Smith, Ralph Straus, Hugh Walpole, Louis Wilkinson and Angus Wilson; and Colin Wilson too, whose *Origins of the Sexual Impulse* makes important contacts with Powys's esoteric sexology.

It is true that Powys throughout his life preserved a certain scepticism on all ultimate issues; but the greater powers were always breaking through. When the grand period of composition came on him after the first world-war, we can feel an inrush, like that of waters breaking down a dam, shattering the veilings and reservations of his first attempt at self-revelation in the 1916 *Confessions of Two Brothers,* an essay which makes an interesting comparison when set beside the *Autobiography* of 1933. The ambivalence, though here extreme, is characteristic. Powys regularly swerves from positive to negative and from negative to positive, steering a delicate course between mysticism and scepticism, seeming to be dominated by neither while including both. This Powysian ambivalence was neatly suggested to me by a letter of 17 February, 1963 from Mr Laurence Kitchin, who as a boy saw Powys at Corwen :

> He used to say his prayers, in a cloak, at the runic stone in Corwen churchyard, within sight of the old priests' college where I spent several holidays. The Rector's widow, who lived there, knew him. When I was a student she refused to introduce us, in fear of his possible influence on me. This nettled me, as he then seemed a god. As time passed she began holding out an introduction to him as bait,

for I was no longer at leisure to go up to the College for a visit. At last I did make the trip, but was not allowed to meet Powys. By that time she was convinced that *I* would upset *him*.

That is perhaps as good a way as any to define Powys's religious position.

He is deeply and traditionally unorthodox; he is against all ' establishments ' and as sceptical of scepticism as he is of dogma. He remains imaginatively at home, whenever it suits him, with either, while putting his final trust only in those poetic and occult perceptions that have from time immemorial enriched the consciousness of man. In sexual matters, too, he is similarly both unorthodox and traditional, explicitly formulating, though with a number of typical reservations and repudiations, what has for too long remained merely implicit and embedded in our poetic and dramatic traditions : the compulsion on man of the bisexual, or seraphic, vision which, though transmitted through human figures, speaks from a dimension beyond the biological.*

Whereas earlier creative writers kept these occult and seraphic intuitions so well woven into their artistic fabrics that we could at least pretend to ignore them, Powys allows no such opportunity for escape. Like Nietzsche he writes from the beyond - good - and - evil consciousness on the border between art and doctrine where each interpenetrates the other. This border modern criticism, uncertainly swaying between aesthetic appreciation and moral allegiance, finds disturbing. Nevertheless avoidance is becoming impossible. It is moreover the nature of all my own interpretations, which exist along this same territory, to render avoidance impossible : their accomplishment both derives from and enforces occult acceptance, their success in the uncovering of new harmonies having, from my first Shakespearian investigation onwards, depended not on any cleverness of my own but rather on a simple — if you like a *naive* — lack of scepticism, unusual in our time, regarding the more mystical properties of great poetry. The interpretation of Powys's writings is the easier in that so much has already been done by the author himself. For Powys, more than any of his predecessors, was consciously living the great truths housed in literature. We may accordingly expect his works to grow steadily in repute, until their stupendous qualities are known.

---

* My most comprehensive discussion of what I intend by the word ' seraphic ' is presented in the long Epilogue, 'The Seraphic Intuition ', given in the 1962 re-issue of *The Christian Renaissance*. The reiteration of occult and bisexual themes throughout British drama is discussed in *The Golden Labyrinth*.

I have, with one exception, attempted to cover only the prose books, which are enough for the present volume. It is good news that Mr Kenneth Hopkins has in preparation a selection from Powys's poetry. I regret not having been able to incorporate duplicate page references to the new edition of *Jobbler Skald* at present in the press with Messrs Macdonald & Co, who have so excellently supported Powys during recent years, under the original American title *Weymouth Sands;* though I confess that I myself like the original title less than the one to which I have grown accustomed and which seems so well to suit that powerful story. I have, apart from *Rodmoor* which was not published in England, used English editions, and my page numerals apply to these; but I have given chapter numerals also to facilitate reference to other editions and translations, now and in the future. Except where specifically noted, my dates are those of the English editions, most of which appeared within a year of the American publication.

I am grateful to Mr E. E. Bissell for lending me a copy of *Rodmoor* from his rich collection of Powysiana; to Mr Oliver Campion for many helpful discussions on Powys and for driving me to Blaenau-Ffestiniog in his car; to Mr V. P. Underwood for telling me of Mr Garma C. C. Chang's *Teachings of Tibetan Yoga;* to Mr Kenneth Young, who has himself written powerfully on Powys, and to Mr W. T. Oliver, for their collaboration in support of Powys through the columns of *The Yorkshire Post;* and to Mr Maurice Barbanell for his, through those of *Psychic News;* to Miss Frances Horsfield for the evidence of Powys's survival referred to on p. 129 below; and to Mr John Foster White and Messrs Macdonald & Co (Publishers) Ltd for numerous favours, including permission to use on the wrapper of this volume the photograph by the Madoc Studio of Powys receiving the Plaque of the Free Academy of Arts in Hamburg.

My obligations to Mr Derek Langridge are many. Not only do I owe to him the impulse towards the composition of this volume, but after reading my script he drew attention to the poem ' The Saturnian ' which so neatly supports my central emphasis that I have used an extract from it on my title page. He it was, too, who told me of the fascinating passage, which I quote below (p. 128), by the kind permission of Messrs E. P. Dutton & Co, Inc, from W. E. Woodward's *The Gift of Life;* and both he and Dr Bernard Jones have helped me on points of topography.

Finally, I would thank Miss Phyllis Playter, not only for giving me permission to dedicate this study to her, but also for her many kindnesses on my visits to Corwen and Blaenau-Ffestiniog, and in correspondence. Letters from Powys to myself are, through the kind collaboration of the keeper, Mr B. S. Page, being privately lodged in the Brotherton Collection at the University of Leeds.

For page references to my present volume I use the letter ' p '; for references to other books, numerals only.

G.W.K.

Exeter; September, 1963

An unavoidable further delay in publication has enabled me to add a few names to my preface and to incorporate some new passages in my final chapter. Meanwhile I have, for the first time for many years, visited Weymouth, and also Portland, which I was surprised to find invisible from Weymouth. The Portland visit considerably enriched my understanding of *Jobber Skald,* and made me wonder whether ' *Portland Stone* ' would not have been a better alternative title than ' *Weymouth Sands* '. After that I saw the Cerne Giant in all his glory. For help in tracing the books containing descriptions and pictures of him (noted on p. 22 below) I am indebted to Mr and Mrs Francis Berry.

The purely literary analyses of this study necessarily attempt no indication of the spiritual powers — the generosity, the humour, the sun-like warmth — of Powys's own giant personality. Those who never knew him may receive much from the wonderful letters to Louis Wilkinson. For the rest, my brief essay ' Homage to Powys ', to be included by Mr Kenneth Young in the new collection of *Yorkshire Post* articles entitled *The Second Bed Post* (Macdonald & Co), must for the present serve, however inadequately, as my tribute.

I have to thank Miss Olive Mordue for assistance in proof-reading and the checking of my indexes.

G.W.K.

Exeter; August, 1964

CHAPTER I
The Poetic Core

The word ' poet ' may be hard to define, but its most valuable use is, as Shelley saw, comprehensive. If we want a sharper definition, we may turn to Powys's *A Glastonbury Romance:*

> What's Poetry if it isn't something that has to fight for the unseen against the seen, for the dead against the living, for the mysterious against the obvious?
> (XVII, 549 or 529)

In that there is much truth, though it may not be the whole truth. Poetry is close to myth and it is saturated both in the past and in a consciousness that outspaces the day to day perceptions of contemporary man. We may accordingly call John Cowper Powys a great modern poet using his own insights and his inheritance from past centuries for a modern purpose. He has, it is true, won fame chiefly by his series of ' novels ', but the term scarcely suits them, since it was made for a particular kind of social and sexual fiction arising in the seventeenth century and appealing to a particular class and a particular time. The very word suggests the ' new ', and therefore the ephemeral; whereas Powys is more at home with what is age-old and enduring.

A good key to his life-work is the blank-verse narrative *Lucifer,* written in 1905 but not published until 1956. Its hero Lucifer, rebel against God, is in the Renaissance tradition of theological revolt which gave us the Faust and Don Juan myths, Milton's Satan and Blake's poetic thought. These Renaissance revolutionaries are usually, like Byron's Lucifer in *Cain,* expressions of modern instincts and modern reasoning. But Powys, taking in also the great stream of Hellenic mythology that has done so much to inspire Renaissance culture, shows his hero as searching within a non-Hebraic mythology for satisfaction. Never before have these twin powers of our culture, the Satanic and the Hellenic, been so purposively combined. But since Powys is nothing if not comprehensive, his Lucifer, after approaching the Earth-Goddess, Pan and Dionysus, finally visits Buddha, so that the religious consciousness of the East is also contained, if only, in this

17

instance, to be rejected. Meanwhile God is weakening; favour falls on youth and young love; and social revolution, honoured though inadequate, before it fails entangles a Red Flag to the arm of a figured Christ. Finally Lucifer wills his great Cosmopolis, his ' City of the Sun ' (IV), regains his pristine splendour and challenges futurity. This is our conclusion :

> He spoke and raised his hands and stretched them forth,
> Moulding the night air in impassioned palms;
> As though like potter's clay the future slept
> Between them. Then with unmoved face he turned
> Contemptuous, and strode back, and made himself
> Mist in the mist. The dark rock-promontory
> Once more hung lonely. One by one the stars
> Rose, and took up their station. With the same
> Bright callousness they rose, as when at first
> Men named them stars. Their rising swept the Earth
> Into its rightful place of littleness;
> And o'er the heads of gods and giants swung,
> In patient unperturbed indifference,
> The punctual planets; and the planets above,
> In pride yet haughtier, marched the Milky Way.

(VI)

Lucifer does more than contain embryonically the potential of Powys's subsequent writing; it is, in itself, not only a fine poem but a valuable attempt to place our age within the context of the centuries. That Powys should have afterwards turned to prose was wise. What he had to say would have had less impact in poetic form; it would have been either limited to an aesthetic approbation or denigrated by tendentious criticism. The imponderables concerned, at once so simple and so remote, demanded expression through a less sophisticated medium capable of every needed modulation from the trivial to the tremendous.

His mental storehouse includes those successors to ancient myth and orthodox religion, the great writers of our Western tradition. In *Visions and Revisions* (New York 1915; London, revised, 1955) and *The Pleasures of Literature* (1938; as *Enjoyment of Literature,* with variations, New York, 1938) he discusses those writers who have meant most to him, such as Homer and Shakespeare, Rabelais, Cervantes, Goethe, Whitman, Melville, Dostoievsky, and Dickens. He spent a large part of his maturity lecturing on these and others, in England and America.

Myths, religions and literature seethe within Powys's ' Pair Dadeni ' or ' Cauldron of Rebirth '. ' Rebirth ' means what it says : Powys looks back before looking forward. Just as Lucifer had to regain his old resplendence before pressing on to his Cosmopolis, so Powys searches in the mists of antiquity for the buried splendour of that golden age whose lord was Cronos, or Saturn.

Powys's control of this expansive imaginative territory comes from his having himself experienced the experiences which it records; and what he is really doing is to call on his great precursors, as occasion suits, for ratification of his own multitudinous insights. His genius might be defined, in distinction from that of earlier sages, as 'Protean '.

There is nevertheless a core to it, which may be called ' Wordsworthian '. On Wordsworth's doctrine Powys once wrote that he had ' nourished ' his ' inner life for more than sixty years ' (*Obstinate Cymric*, 1947; X, 164). Of this doctrine our most comprehensive definition comes in a long verse-fragment contained in Wordsworth's Preface to *The Excursion*. In it he claims to by-pass the Miltonic machinery of Jehovah and his angelic hosts and penetrate a greater secret ' to which the heaven of heavens is but a veil '; and this greater secret lies in ' the Mind of Man ' which he calls ' my haunt, and the main region of my song '. Old myths of Paradise and Elysian Fields ' sought in the Atlantic Main ' are symbolic gestures towards an experience within human compass :

> For the discerning intellect of Man,
> When wedded to this goodly universe
> In love and holy passion, shall find these
> A simple produce of the common day.
> — I, long before the blissful hour arrives,
> Would chant, in lonely peace, the spousal verse
> Of this great consummation.

He proclaims

> How exquisitely the individual Mind
> (And the progressive powers perhaps no less
> Of the whole species) to the external World
> Is fitted : — and how exquisitely, too —
> Theme this but little heard of among men —
> The external World is fitted to the Mind;
> And the creation (by no lower name
> Can it be called) which they with blended might
> Accomplish : this is our high argument.

Especially important are the words ' wedded ', ' lonely ', ' spousal ', and ' progressive '. There is a love-union of mind and matter; the evolutionary thought looks ahead to a greater humanity; and it is emphasised that the external world is strangely ' fitted ' to mental action, as though it were itself of mental or semi-mental stuff. This is the best definition of Wordsworth's nature-mysticism.

For the understanding of Powys we need to supplement it by a couple of lines on soul-projection from Coleridge's *France: an Ode,* where he claims to have

> shot my being through earth, sea, and air,
> Possessing all things with intensest love . . .

Our Wordsworthian and Coleridgean quotations are together covered by Andrew Marvell's *The Garden,* wherein the poet first enjoys objective nature; next gains a yet greater happiness by creating a mind-nature dissolving the external world into the unitary sensation of ' a green Thought in a green Shade '; and finally projects his soul, liberated from its body's ' vest ', into external nature, which has now regained its rights, the soul sitting like a bird and singing in a tree. These experiences are regarded as a liberation from social and sexual complexities and culminate in thoughts of *solitary* bliss in Eden's golden age before Eve's arrival and the Fall.

Since myth and poetry appear to arise from a marriage of mind and matter in which the barrier between the ego and its environment is removed and man becomes free within a living and personal, or personalised, universe, our three quotations might be said to distil their essence. And since Powys's many descriptions of his own experiences read like an expanded commentary on these quotations, we find that the doctrine he derives from them is not merely a poetic doctrine but *the doctrine of poetry.* What he counsels directly and indirectly in both his fiction and his teaching is what he sometimes calls ' elementalism '. He urges us to cultivate the Wordsworthian power of feeling into the inanimate; to enjoy all nature, and especially its less obviously living manifestations, such as earth, stone, wind and sea, not haphazardly but by an act of will. Sometimes he says that any object, even any human artefact, will do, all that is needed being the embrace by the ego of the external world. Sometimes he visualises the soul as being projected from the physical body, like Marvell's silver bird.

On occasion he appears to regard the elements as themselves conscious but sometimes, and especially when thinking of old buildings, walls and paths, he regards past human associations as playing their part. Past human emotions can be impressed on localities. Like Wordsworth in so many passages of *The Prelude,* Powys has a sense of a haunting past, and also of parental or ancestral spirits; and in looking for what Wordsworth called the ' Elysian Fields ' he is always likely to search *back* in racial history to a lost Golden Age, such as was supposed in classical mythology to have existed under Saturn, or Cronos, before the present dispensation.

This mind-nature fusion is regarded by Powys as a kind of sexual union, having its own ' sensuality'; and correspondingly in its approach to human beings the Powysian sexology is strangely *impersonal*. Both in what he tells us of himself and in the many self-reflections in his novels there is a divergence from ordinary desire to a more refined but impersonal and cerebral fascination, seeing girls, again in Wordsworthian fashion (p. 61), as elemental beings such as sylphs or undines; while boys or youths — there are already premonitions of it in *Lucifer* — hold the seraphic radiations customary in poetry and drama.* Powys writes from a bisexual integration finding in such figures as these intimations of some ' Saturnian ' (pp. 60-1) sex beyond male and female. Himself, as he tells us, half a woman, he is a Tiresias understanding sexual affairs from the woman's side; but since they are so subjectively approached his fictional women arc, unless of a type that has male or bisexual extensions, less individualised than his men. Male friendship, sometimes with reminders of his brother Llewelyn, is emphatic.

He never forgets that there are horrors too awful for any theology to explain or any teaching to assuage. He knows in himself the sadistic instinct; he sees it active in others, especially in vivisection; and he finds it implanted in the universal scheme. Much of his writing can be read as an attempt to replace this grim recognition by a sunnier, more kindly and more humorous, gospel, searching for a life-way such as he believes may have existed in antiquity. More and more he relies on the ancient literature of Wales in which, deep below the horrors which it faces and understands, he contends that the Saturnian secret lies embedded. One great question, the question of Death and human survival, he attacks, in book after book; he is obsessed by it. His elemental and spiritualistic intuitions and experiences open manifold possibilities; and if, as he thinks, we are wiser to

---

* These I have discussed in *Christ and Nietzsche*, 1948, IV; *The Christian Renaissance*, edn. of 1962, ' Epilogue '; and throughout *The Golden Labyrinth*, 1962.

think less of a universe than of a multiverse, the chances and possibilities are only multiplied. Nevertheless, he grows, as the years pass, more doubtful. Even so, while his explicit thought remains agnostic, his objective art becomes less and less earth-bound, steering finally sun-ward an astral, or etheric, course.

Throughout his guiding symbol, signifying the gigantic powers and violences of sexual instincts and aberrations, is the phallically excited and cudgel-wielding Cerne Giant of Cerne Abbas in Dorset.* Mr John M. Wood tells us that according to Celtic tradition Britain was peopled after the Flood by ' men of great heart and strength ' designated as ' *cedeirn* ', meaning ' mighty ones ' or ' giants ' (J. M. Wood, ' In Search of The Real King Arthur '; *Anthroposophical Quarterly*, VII, 2; Summer, 1962; 37). Despite all apparent dangers, the adulatory tone of the phrase ' of great heart and strength ' will, before we have concluded our study, be found not irrelevant to Powys's favourite giant.

---

* A full discussion, with a number of illustrations, of the Cerne Giant is given by Morris Marples in *White Horses and other Hill Figures* (1949). Brief accounts, with illustrations, occur in Ralph Dutton's *Wessex* (1949) and Eric Benfield's *Dorset* (1950).

CHAPTER II
Early Narratives

The Novels may be called expansions of Powys's personal experiences into a more generalised and objective survey. Widely considered, the integration of man and nature is not easy; nature often seems evil; the integration has to be arduously won. We shall now turn to his first three narratives, published before the famous sequence starting with *Wolf Solent*.

Using a Dorset setting *Wood and Stone* (USA, 1915; London, 1917), a long tale of swiftly flowing lucidity, contrasts Nevilton Mount and its Christian associations with Leo's Hill, a ' tawny Monster ' (I, 3) marked by earth-works dating back to pre-Celtic times and now a quarry for valuable stone. The hill's pagan associations and spiritual presences and agencies are throughout regarded as evil, the more so since it and its elemental wealth are owned by the power-craving, deplorable, and yet courageous, for Powys is always generous to such people, Mortimer Romer. Romer enjoys tyrannising over the stoically ineffectual and eccentric Mr Quincunx. His daughter Gladys is cruel as her father; both have sadistic strains, and Gladys's subtle tormenting of the girl Lacrima is a brilliant psychological study.

Natural descriptions are throughout sinister. Though wood is contrasted with stone as good against evil (XVII, 440; XVIII, 463), the stone and its companion the ' malignantly clinging ' (XII, 262) clay dominate. Moreover, other natural descriptions, including vegetation (XIV, 326), are unpleasantly toned.

The most moving character is James Anderson, a strong and likable carver, forecast of the Jobber in *Jobber Skald*, who has grown to love the stone of Leo's Hill, which has become part of him (XVII, 440; XVIII, 463). He dies on the hill. His younger brother Luke, beautiful as a ' Greek God ' (I, 12), is drawn from Powys's brother Llewelyn. Death is in Powys a pervading theme but never elsewhere so poignant as when Luke sits by the mystery of his brother's corpse.

Luke's beauty is vivid, and so is Gladys's. When costumed as Ariadne in Greek style, dressed in ' gentian blue ' with short skirt and 'boyish sandals', she becomes 'a Sunchild', an elemental creature 'of air and earth and fire', bathing the whole world 'in translucent and unclouded ether' (XI, 243, 239). Her evil is constituent to a personality which touches bisexual grace.

In *Wood and Stone* essences which are to be handled and rehandled later are present under an ambiguous and distrustful survey. Gladys's excellence is one with her danger; James may have made terms with stone, but we are aware of 'the fatal force of Inanimate Objects over human destiny' and of the evils radiating from a pagan past (I, 3). Earth-nature is throughout unfriendly. But light comes from Weymouth, where our plot-problems are resolved, and Luke's 'slim golden figure' catches the 'horizontal sunlight' before he strikes out 'for the open sea' (XXII, 589).

And yet in *Rodmoor* (1916) the North Sea is our evil principle. We are in East Anglia. The sea is sinister. Its recurring sound is maddening and its tides 'godless'. It has already won from the land, submerging human habitations and robbing people of the moral stability given by ancestral presences, and that is why the inhabitants 'have won for themselves a sinister reputation for impiety and perversity' (XXIII, 360). The desolate fens strike terror. Nature's malignancy expresses itself in dark clouds, pitiless winds, and a weird storm. But the north-west wind brings air from sweet earth; earth, not sea is man's proper habitation and the 'horror of the sea' (XIV, 191) is countered by remembrance of the beautiful East Anglian gardens, which correspond to man's moral valuations as does the sea to inroads of unholy instinct. Perversions are feared. Brand Renshaw is a massive study in dark, mysterious, evil, forecasting *A Glastonbury Romance*. Rachel Doorm is the first of Powys's dark women. Instead of the swift-flowing narrative of *Wood and Stone,* the prevailing quality is dramatic. The atmosphere is sensational and suspense is keen.

The hero Adrian Sorio, with his heavy stick, is the first of Powys's succession of obvious — the reservation is needed — self-reflections, whom we shall henceforward call the 'Powys-hero'. He has been in an asylum in America, and is composing a book on destruction as the key to existence. But the 'nothingness' of death is only a name 'for *what lies beyond life*', 'beyond the point where every living thing ceases to exist and *becomes nothing*'; it is as a 'blinding white light', and yet the word 'light' is inaccurate, since the otherness extinguishes both light and shadows, itself neither light nor darkness but just ' large and cool and deep and empty '. Adrian's idealised son Baptiste, whom he has left in America, is its ' angel ', and there they will be united (XXI, 324-6; and see VIII, 113).

Adrian is free to marry and loves two girls, Nance and Philippa. Nance is gentle and normal; Philippa, who interrupts his engagement to Nance, abnormal and dangerous.

Philippa, of a type resembling Gladys in *Wood and Stone,* is a boyish-looking girl with a man's brain in a girl's body (III, 46; IV, 49-50; VIII, 114), and like Gladys has a cruel strain. Though resembling some ' delicate evocation of perverse pagan desire ' she has qualities belonging to the Christian era, being like an ' elf-creature ' of medieval magic. She visits the nocturnal woods desiring to be embraced by the elemental powers. She and Adrian had first loved by the — for once — sunlit sea, which had ' mingled their souls '. But for the most part ' this furtive child of marsh and sea ' is felt as growing from, and personifying, the more sinister elements in nature, and is associated with witchcraft (IV, 50-1; VI, 85; VIII, ' Sun and Sea ', 102-117; XXVII, 448; VI, 85; XVII, 237). In her the bisexual charm is vivid and dangerous. We are warned by the wise Mrs Renshaw that a girl should not try to be ' boyish '; God's scheme must be followed, for ' anything else leads to untold wretchedness '; and Dr Raughty levels a forceful indictment against sexual perversions (XVIII, 256; XXII, 345).

And yet their power is insistent. Early in his story Adrian had a vision of a figure neither boy nor girl but possessing ' the nature of both ' :

> It gazed at me with a fixed, sorrowful stare, and I felt — was not that a strange experience — that I had known it before, somewhere, far off, and long ago.

Its expression held both ' tragic supplication ' and ' mockery '. It was the kind of form

> that one can imagine wandering in vain helplessness down all the years of human history, seeking amid the dreams of all the great, perverse artists of the world for the incarnation it has been denied by the will of God.
>
> (I, 18)

Despite Nance's battle for Adrian's mental safety, his end is with, or near, the bisexual Philippa.

But Baptiste is his true soul-mate. He alone draws near to Adrian's secret. We have heard of his ' sweetness ', of his long lashes lying on his cheek when he sleeps; and he is the ' angel ' of Adrian's Nirvana (VI, 85; XXI, 323, 326). When Nance sends for him from America to restore Adrian's mind, she imagines him on the ship ' like a young god ', and the boy visits her dreams as a figure of ' unearthly beauty ' and ' supernatural power ' (XXVI, 433).

As Adrian towards the close goes by night with Philippa towards the sea he feels awaiting him an image ' moulded of white mists and white vapours and the reflection of white stars in dark waters '; all part of some vast and elemental infinitude beyond human manifestations, beyond both life *and* death, a ' Nothingness ' that is an ' escape ' and a ' refuge ' dwarfing humanity and its gods. He eludes Philippa, he smells the sea, and before winning death within the star-kissed waters, his last cry is ' Baptiste ' (XXVII, 456-8). So subtly does Powys blend bisexual love and the seraphic ideal with sea and death and the white mystery beyond.

Rodmoor dramatises its hero's union with the apparently perverse and the apparently hostile. But the rights of normality remain in Nance's suffering goodness, and the wise old Mrs Renshaw, exponent of a feminine wisdom, asserts normality and the abilities of women to enjoy and sanctify trivial tasks in a way that forecasts Powys's latest, Homeric, thinking : ' God has given to these little things a peculiar consecration ' (XVIII, 252).

In *Ducdame* (1925) we feel Powys leaving swift narrative and dramatic suspense for the more metaphysically weighted manner which he is henceforward to adopt and develop.

We are back in Dorset. In *Rodmoor* the numinous was identified with the sea which had drowned the ancestral earth-ghosts, but here those ghosts are alive and active, willing with Mrs Ashover that her son, Rook Ashover, should marry and beget an heir to carry on his ancient line. His ancestors, whose monuments are in the local church, are on her side, for the dead will their own perpetuation and deep below ' the slow dissolution of the centuries ' there is a power beyond ' annihilation ' (XIII, 188). Graves we had in *Wood and Stone;* here they are less graves than powers. Sensations descend to us from our parents and earlier, and past human emotions are impressed on places. Our ground is saturated with history. When the ancestral will for Rook is to be consummated, he, as by second sight, sees through pitch darkness the *whiteness* of the snow-covered ground and hears an uncanny sound from the exulting dead (IX, 123-5). Once the ghost-face of Rook's cavalier ancestor Sir Robert actually appears.

Rook, a typical ' Powys-hero ', is ill-at-ease with women. Like James in *Wood and Stone* he has a younger brother, again like Powys's brother Llewelyn, who is dying. These two younger brothers find sexual accomplishment easy, but Rook endures attractions without emotion; he wishes he could have his love-affairs with trees or the elements (X, 139; XX, 300-2; XXIII, 384). However, life and his ancestors have their way; he is manoeuvred into marrying Lady Ann, a Viking-descended, athletic, horse-loving and hunting successor to Gladys and Philippa, conceived as a militant representative of the life-force (XXIV, 409-20); and a child is coming.

Rook's ancestors are opposed by Mr Hastings, the Vicar of Ashover, a man of ' enormous magnetism ', almost a ' magician ' (X, 140; XVIII, 285-6; XXIV, 414; IV, 55), who regards life as loathsome and is writing a yet darker book than Adrian's, which is regarded by everyone as evil. Like Adrian, he loves an infinite ' Nothingness ' (XIV, 197, 210); he claims to have discovered the secret of Destruction, the ' anti-vital energy ' (X, 144), by which he would give man power to counteract God's creativeness. Death is not enough; he wants to ' stop death from breeding life ' by getting behind ' both life and death ' to the ' mainspring ' by a process of ' cosmic unravelling ', like the ' unwinding ' of a ' clock '. He asserts a soul-power able to open the sluices and let death flood life and to this end regards his book as a ' magical engine of destruction ' (X, 144; XI, 152; XVIII, 287; XXII, 367; XXIV, 413). Hastings forecasts Uryen Quirm in *Maiden Castle*, and also Morsimmon Esty in *The Inmates* who is to be shown actually exerting the unwinding power at which Hastings aims (p. 84 below).

Hastings hates the coming child of the Ashovers and in a frenzy murders Rook, who had already seen his death forecast in the old fortune-teller Betsy's crystal. Rook has other psychic experiences, one of which we have recorded. When most tormented he can project his soul far into nature for solace (VI, 82). He actually meets his unborn son as a handsome youth on horseback, coming as a ghost from the future to comfort his distraught father, and speaking lovingly with a smile ' the penetrating sweetness of which diffused itself through every fibre of the man's body ', his face possessing ' a beauty and power in it beyond anything he had ever approached ' (XIX, 310;

and see XIX, 307-11; XX, 328; XXII, 359; XXV, 433-4). The boy corresponds to the seraphic Baptiste of *Rodmoor*.

Though a numinous atmosphere pervades, it flowers from an earthly setting. Whereas Powys's later tendency is to concentrate more on his favourite, lower, life-forms, we have here an unusually varied and impersonal assortment of flowers, birds and animal-life, of all that Richard Jefferies meant by ' wood-magic '. Nature is manifested in various seasons and in differing moods, but the prevailing effect is one of beneficence, and again and again description rises to a sense of nature blending, by night or day under sun, moon or stars, into some more ' etherealized chemistry ' making a semi-mental world more beautiful than ours (I, 3), its ' pearl-gray mist ' reaching to some ' ghost garden beyond death ' (I, 14-15). Scenes are ' enchanted ' (XVI, 237); gravestones are ' gray rocks in a green halcyon sea ' (XVI, 238); a swan floats as though ' on some mysterious inner lake ' behind or within the actuality (XX, 330); heat-waves arouse intimations of a mystic city (XXI, 337); a cedar's branches swim in air as though floating on blue mist (XXIV, 403). Even mankind share in the blessedness : ' there seemed to float a sort of ideal luminosity, enhancing their dignity, their beauty, their originality, their human worth ' (XXV, 432). Rook listens to old Betsy's talk of her ' Cimmery Land ' :

'Tis real wet rain, what's finer than corpse dust, them folks do live under; and they tell I it be wonderful strange to see 'un walk and talk . . . mum . . . mum . . . mum . . . and thik mist all slivery and dimsy round 'un.

(XVII, 264)

Her disjointed fragments he interprets as confused reports of some real Elysian Fourth Dimension ' where large and liberating thoughts moved to and fro over cool, wet grass like enormous swallows ' (XVII, 264).

In such descriptions the mind-nature opacity is being broken, or dissolved; and in experiences of this dissolution, Rook attains liberation from his torments. Meanwhile, despite Hastings' dark purposes, Ann destroys his manuscript and the child is born.

Ducdame is notable for its realisation of ancestral powers and a strong woman as agents of life; for our first Powys study of a dark magician, here a theologian and in part repudiated but later to gain in authority; and for its pervading sense of earth-nature etherealised blending into sense of an etheric dimension.

In Powys's following books we shall find him wrestling with the more dangerous powers of these first adventures: the pagan stone, heavy earth and clinging fecundities of *Wood and Stone;* the dark sea and perverted instincts of *Rodmoor;* the evils in Brand Renshaw and William Hastings; and the ambiguous bisexuality of Gladys and Philippa. Once again only, in *Jobber Skald,* does he offer so exquisite a sense of nature etherealised as in *Ducdame.* The seraphic ideal, as in Baptiste and Rook's son, is to remain a star.

CHAPTER III

The Famous Narratives

Our exploration is very largely an exploration of the human psyche in interaffective relationship with natural surroundings; and this relationship accumulates new importance in the weighty narratives starting with *Wolf Solent* (1929; 1961). The stories are inevitably less free and forward. The interest centres primarily on this deep relation. Whereas *Ducdame* continually *described* the interaction of scene and mind, *Wolf Solent* is, as a whole, written as *from* that very interaction. We experience throughout from the hero's subjective centre; earth and its vegetations are by him inwardly apprehended, their soul-sap touched, almost as from their own subjective centre; sometimes the mind itself creates its own nature, sometimes external nature becomes less an aggregate of objects than a suffusing and vaporous presence. Human thoughts and instincts are imagistically equated with animal-life or other natural manifestations and human events appear almost to form themselves like steaming vapour rising from the soil. The soul is regarded less as a hard core to the personality than as an enveloping lake or cloud (XIX, 454 or 433; XXIV, 602 or 574). And yet there is no loss of solidity; we are in an earth-world and a world of thick vegetation; but that earth-world's solidity is itself mysterious. The solid and the atmospheric are in strange identity.

The scene is Dorset, near the Somerset boundary, in and between Ramsgard (Sherborne) and Blacksod (Yeovil). ' Blacksod ', together with the ' Vale of Blackmore ', suggests a darkly-toned pastoralism, fecund without being idyllic. Though there is no all-dominating assertion of the fearsome, natural phenomena are suffused by a prevailing melancholy; arboreal vegetation, rain, river and pond are variously fascinating and oppressive. The colour-tone is of green blending into grey. Lenty Pond is sinister, and so is Jason's Hindu idol Muk-a-Log, the rain god. The atmosphere is, we might say, damp, or if sunny, we are more likely to be aware of heavy afternoon heat than of keen airs and dawn. Sunset may be ominous :

The sun was so low now that he could look straight into its great red circle suspended above the roofs of the town. It resembled, as he looked at it, a vast fiery tunnel, the mouth of some colossal piece of artillery, directed full against him. With screwed-up eyelids he returned the stare of this blood-red cannon-mouth; and as he fronted it, it seemed to him that a dusky figure took shape within it, a figure resembling Jason Otter's abominable idol.

(VI, 266 or 251)

For much of the story nature is muffled by darkness; or we may be indoors by lamp or candle-light. Partly by contrast to this prevalent sobriety, both flowers and birds, though there were as many numerically in *Ducdame,* are here more richly apprehended. Earthly odours, from pig-stye to flower-scent, are heavy. Earth is prodigal of both evil and good, the home of mouldering corpses and the cradle of buttercups. By day or night, it is confronted by clouds and sky; earth and sky are here as two vast creatures in mutual regard.

From this atmospheric soil grow our people and all their strange undergrowths of instinct and sensation and the leafage of half-formed thoughts and half-recognised purposes. Humanity is entangled, or identified, with nature. The blackbird-fluting of the earth-girl Gerda is one expression of this identity, and the three haunting lyrics of the poet Jason are another.

Gerda is loved and married by Wolf, the hero, who has come to replace the deceased young Redfern as secretary to the mysteriously evil Squire Urquhart. Gerda has earth-lore and animal-lore (XVIII, 385 or 367); she is called an ' oread ' (X, 241 or 226); when her fluting comes from a tree we may be reminded of Rima in W. H. Hudson's *Green Mansions,* but she is less ideally conceived, being a very ordinary country girl, as real and convincing as the earth itself.

Like Adrian Sorio in *Rodmoor* Wolf loves two girls, Gerda and Christie. Gerda is physically felt; Christie, daughter of the bookseller Malakite, is more spiritual. She is called variously elphish or elphin, an air-spirit or Ariel, a sylph; she is silvery, virginal and remote; almost sexless or androgynous (IV, 80 or 71), successor to Philippa Renshaw, only more delicately conceived. Her speaking is as of some ' half-human personality . . . some changeling out of the purer elements ' (IX, 224 or 210). She suggests a priestess of some remote goddess, perhaps Artemis (V, 85 or 76); she is also related to the Christian element in Arthurian legend, whereas Gerda's lineage — though she is also called a ' Saxon ' (X, 237 or 222) — is more ancient (XV, 330 or 314). But there are sinister elements in Christie's background. Her father sells evil books, has had a child Olwen by another daughter, and finally makes advances to Christie herself. She loves Sir Thomas Browne's sepulchral *Hydriotaphia,* or *Urn Burial,* and is herself planning a book on dangerous themes, to be called ' *Slate* ' (XX, 459 or 437). There is a dark power in her, such as Powys associates with Wales; her mother was Welsh and claimed descent from Merlin (X, 248 or 233); and ' Slate ' is a Welsh mineral.

There is power too in the child Olwen, who while on a merry-go-round is struck by thwarted jealousy :

> Two burning eyes flashed down at him like two quivering poniards, and two fierce little hands clutched the sides of the olive-green boat as if they had been the sides of a war-chariot . . .
>
> (IX, 214 or 201)

So the little girl, helplessly orbiting in her tiny green vehicle, ' whirled ' past him like an ' angry-eyed comet '. The description makes a cameo of destiny, human and cosmic.

Squire Urquhart, whom Wolf has to help to compose a malicious book on Dorsetshire scandals, is a figure of Gothic wickedness arising from the ' abysmal ooze ' and ' slime ' deeper — as Brand Renshaw claimed for *his* evil (p. 24) — than anything we normally imagine (IX, 186 or 174). He suffers a mysterious unrest concerning the beautiful Redfern whom he had apparently loved and who had died of pneumonia after what seems to have been an attempt at suicide in Lenty Pond. By night he digs up the grave. The embittered poet Jason had also loved Redfern. A strong element of homosexuality is written into *Wolf Solent.* Our thought on such perversions pursues a moral border-line. Repudiatory hints of evil may be countered by the action. When, in a scene of exquisite and half-humorous penetration Urquhart and Jason together watch the admirably characterised youth Bob Weevil and the boy Lobby Torp bathing in Lenty Pond, their evil falls from them like masks, the Gothic monster suddenly becoming an enthusiastic schoolmaster and the Satanic poet an ' enraptured saint ', their ' every ounce of black bile or complicated evil ' having been drawn off by the boys' ' classic nakedness '. Indeed the Squire's ' purged and almost hieratic look ' awakes ' a warm salt tide ' of sympathy in us which threatens, as from a sea-realm beyond human dualisms, our ethical embankments (XIV, 300-2 or 284-6).

Wolf is tugged and distraught by his own instincts and the encompassing powers and people, among them his dominating mother, the wise Selena Gault and the subtly drawn cleric T. E. Valley. Sometimes it seems that Wolf himself is of a type similar to Urquhart and Jason, and that male friendship means more to him than a woman's love (XXII, 531 or 506; XXIII, 566, or 539). Once, aware of a Lesbian attachment between two girls, he enjoys a sense of keen yet darkly-dangerous fascination (XVIII, 404-6 or 385-8). He can be attracted by evil books, though their exact nature is not defined; and he is tormented by human suffering. He often senses his dead father's presence and thinks continually of his body mouldering in its grave. He is of an introverted disposition and his most cherished possession is what he calls his 'mythology', which started in his childhood at Weymouth (I, 15-16, or 7; XIX, 434 or 413). This is a mystical-sensuous enjoyment given connotations of both moral conflict (XIX, 431 or 411) and viciousness, and described variously in imagery of sub-marine fish-life and vegetation in greenish depths (II, 35 or 27; XIX, 420 or 401; 434 or 414; XXI, 513-4 or 489; XXIII, 552 or 526). It is called 'Cimmerian' and may point towards some mystic soul-city (II, 29 or 20; VII, 168-9 or 157).

Like other Powys-heroes, he carries a heavy stick, but he is sexually more successful than most, his marriage to Gerda being, even if it is mainly confined to 'dalliance' (XII, 280 or 263), provisionally successful, though it is the abnormal Christie who touches, as Gerda does not, his inmost identity. Christie allows his approaches. A suffusing greenish light from the lamp-shade helps to identify Christie with Wolf's submarine mythology; and the point at issue is whether he shall express it in physical union. He does not. He fails her. Does her Artemis-personality repel advance? Or is he an inhibited weakling? Both of them have repudiated Platonism (XVI, 357 or 340); and yet what exactly *is* this love? Would sexual action be a desecration? This is how it happens:

> There came a moment's sinking into nothingness, into a grey gulf of non-existence; and then it was as if a will within him, that was beyond thought, gathered itself together in that frozen chaos and rose upwards — rose upwards like a shining-scaled fish, electric, vibrant, taut, and leapt into the greenish-coloured vapour that filled the room!

(XX; 466 or 444)

The fish is in this book a mystical symbol of the 'Unutterable', once a symbol of Christ (XXI, 510 or 486, 516 or 492). The image grows from the room's green luminance.

Christie is human enough to feel slighted. Subsequently after having apparently been submissive to the lust of her father, now dead

— he says that she killed him — she deliberately aligns herself with
her evil associations rather than Wolf :

> 'Damn you ! ' she cried. 'Damn you! You talking fool! You great,
> stupid, talking fool ! What do *you* know of me or my father? What
> do *you* know of my real life?
>
> (XXIV, 606 or 578)

Christie now despises him. Gerda has another lover. Wolf is alone.

Even his 'mythology' has gone, killed it seems by his desecrating
desire for Christie (XIX, 420 or 401; 434 or 414). But he is not
lost. He has had supernal insights, including an important liberation
from disgust at the foulnesses of physical, 'excremental', existence
to a new 'acceptance', though the trouble recurs (XIII, 292-4 or
276-8; XIX, 452-4 or 431-3). He has known, continually, the
Powysian power of projecting his soul into nature (e.g. XIX, 447 or
426). At a key-moment his torment is stilled by the seraphic intuition,
met already in *Rodmoor* and *Ducdame,* of 'a smile of such sheer,
innate sweetness and goodness' on the face of a school-boy, that he
is 'staggered' (XXIV, 589 or 561-2). And now he enjoys a final
revelation.

Wolf Solent often reads like an expansion of Andrew Marvell's
poem *The Garden* (p. 20 above). In both nature functions as a
release from sexual demands. Wolf's 'mythology' corresponds to
Marvell's 'far other worlds and other seas' and the 'green thought
in a green shade' is very obviously recalled when Wolf, his hands on
an elm-tree, tries to evoke the 'master-sensation' of his submarine
mythology :

> With a desperate straining of all the energy of his spirit, he struggled
> to merge his identity in that subaqueous landscape. He had, at that
> moment, a strange feeling, as if he were seeking to embrace in the
> very act of love the maternal earth herself! For, as he strained his
> spirit to the uttermost, the landscape before him ceased to be a mere
> assemblage of contours and colours. It became one enormous water-
> plant, of vast, cool, curving, wet-rooted leaves . . .
>
> (XIX, 434 or 414)

Wolf's experiences of soul-projection correspond to Marvell's silver
soul-bird. Marvell's poem concludes by comparing the state achieved
to loneliness in Eden before Eve's arrival and the Fall. Similarly *Wolf
Solent* concludes with a revelation in solitude which is compared to
the Saturnian Age of Gold.

Inward and outward, 'mythology' and soul-projection, now
coalesce; body and soul are 'coming together' (XXV, 635 or 606).

As Wolf enters a field of brilliant buttercups, the sense of good and evil in conflict, on which his ' mythology' was in part based, has ' vanished '. We are beyond ethic, beyond good and evil. He is in a sea of sunset gold — like the sun on his friend Darnley (XVIII, 395 or 377) — recalling to him the golds in ancient myth and especially the golden, which was Saturn's, age. Thinking of Wordsworth's poetry, Wolf stands enraptured in this field of ' Cimmerian ' or ' Saturnian ' gold. He finds himself living in a new way in and through his body; a strange simplicity is attained. Life will be henceforth not merely accepted but, in all its simplest physical motions, newly enjoyed : ' It's my body that has saved me.' He is, it is true, ' alone ', but aloneness is the inevitable truth (XXV, 638-44 or 609-14). The note is one of attainment, blessedness and courage.

The ancient earth-works of Poll's Camp point back to *Wood and Stone* and on to *Maiden Castle*. The shamelessly phallic chalk-figure of the Dorsetshire Cerne Giant, a key symbol in Powys's thought, finds a natural place among Mr Urquhart's researches; and Mr Malakite's book-shop was in ' Cerne Street ' (XIV, 295 or 279; XVI, 332-3 or 316-7; IV, 59 or 51). From Dorset we look towards Glastonbury Tor and the green-blue haze of Somerset water-meadows (V, 103 or 94; XV, 330 or 314; XVIII, 407 or 388; XXV, 632 or 603; V, 96 or 87). Glastonbury is to be our next scene.

In *Wolf Solent* spirit-powers were, in the main, felt or contained *within* the mind-nature fusion. Mysteries both of nature and of evil were left without distinction and definition. In *A Glastonbury Romance* (1933; 1955) there is a greater variety of defined powers, whether of good or evil, of nature or from beyond. The prevailing colour is blue (e.g. atmospheric, XXI, 694 or 667 and XXX, 1141 or 1089; for Welsh deity, VII, 203 or 210).

Nature is no longer limited to earth and sky as humanly perceived, but ranges the outer spaces wherein the Sun is a conscious agent, hugely and ominously apprehended :

> In the roaring, raving, towering, cresting, cascading whirl of its huge centrifugal flames the superhuman consciousness of that noonday sun recognised, amid the billions upon billions of other organisms that floated through its non-human awareness, his brief-lived biped enemy — the stalwart priest of Christ.
>
> (XII, 328 or 320; and see I, 1 or 21; XIII, 368 or 358)

The Moon, virgin threat to human systems, is felt to exert, throughout one wonderful paragraph, its anarchic witchery (X, 284-5 or 278-80).

Venus, floating in a greenish sky-sea, drops on human anguish a serene comfort (XVII, 559 or 538-9; V, 123 or 135). No antagonist, whether of the astronomical or the psychic universe, is too great for Powys's grappling within this vast compendium of cosmic speculation.

Glastonbury, set among water-meadows, canopied by bluish vapours and soaked in legend, is as a split in earth through which magic may be active. Joseph of Arimathea, Arthur and Merlin are almost living presences; Christian and pre-Christian memories are with us; the Grail is a protagonist. Myth and legend blend into a more general and unmediated occultism. Terms such as ether, aura, clairvoyance, trance, medium, of which there were, for Powys, comparatively few in *Wolf Solent*, pervade. We are on a border-line between spirit and matter : we are reminded that sex-lust is really less physical than psychic (XII, 329-30 or 322); and yet psychic imponderables here have *body*. Thoughts are felt hovering; souls go astral-travelling in sleep; past experience lives in present locality; spirits of the dead are active; the human drama is observed by watchers from another dimension. Mysteries are handled with sharp and stark realism, as in this, of a sudden murder :

> His consciousness, the ' I am I ' of Tom Barter, shot up into the ether above them like a released fountain-jet and quivering there pulsed forth a spasm of feeling, in which outrage, ecstasy, indignation, recognition, pride, touched a dimension of Being more quick with cosmic life than Tom had ever reached before in his thirty-seven years of conscious existence.

(XXIX, 1100 or 1051)

The man's consciousness dissolved, but whether the personal identity passed intact ' into that invisible envelope of rarefied matter which surrounds our astronomic sphere ', or was lost, Powys does not claim, and the thought is repeated for another death (XXX; 1172 or 1118), to know.

The various themes are knitted with as much realism as is humanly possible into a contemporary reading of man's relation to the cosmos.

Our human norm, our ' Powys-hero ', is John Crow from the *Rodmoor* territory of East Anglia. Like Wolf he has his stick, has sense of his dead father's presence, and is no normal lover, his love-making, more closely defined than Wolf's, being of the sterile and cerebral yet wholly satisfying kind usual in these heroes; he is in part homosexual (XVI, 508 or 491). Though he prays to his father and is all but a stone-worshipper at Stonehenge, he remains sceptical of

Glastonbury's mythology even after having psychically experienced a re-activation of history as he sees Arthur's sword plunge into the Brue. The hilt was black, not the legendary golden, the psychometric record being more exact than myth.

There is a pervading eroticism, including a number of aberrations : homosexuality, sadism, masochism, narcissism. Normal sexuality from a woman's experience has never been accorded a finer insight than in the description of Nell Zoyland's preparation for, and enjoyment of, her union with Sam Dekker.

Sam, son of the local priest, is a simple countryman who rejects his love for Nell in obedience to his conception of Christ. The Incarnation he sees at first as an avatar into nature from some wholly other dimension which has since formed part of it (IX, 265 or 260), a thought-line already discussed in *Wood and Stone* (VIII, 153; IX, 165-6); but his beliefs are not all orthodox, his Christ, whose presence he feels as a figure of eternal suffering, being only one among other less beneficent deities (XVI, 481 or 465; XXV, 852 or 815). His use of will-power to crush his natural love of Nell is regarded as a perverted kind of self-negating, alien to the historical Jesus whose spirit tries in vain to deflect him (XVIII, 572-3 or 551-2). However he attains a mystical experience. Inanimate objects are felt as magnetic, as porous, as sources of life (XXVIII, 977-80 or 934-7). The earth seems to crack, he endures what seems like a spear-thrust into his bowels from below, and sees the Grail as a transparent bowl containing a fish (XXVIII, 981-2 or 938-9). When in his saintly course he is ministering to an old man suffering from piles, this anal thrust, his mastery of the repellent, and the Grail, all fuse with his present activity to give hint of

> some incredible secret, whereby the whole massed weight of the
> world's tormented flesh was labouring towards some release.
>
> (XXVIII; 991 or 948)*

His mastery of the repellent repeats Wolf's in *Wolf Solent* where the mystical fish was also forecast (p. 33 above). Henceforth Sam's Christ is less a person than a principle activating all matter; his own soul now, like Wolf's before his Saturnian revelation, both dominates and permeates his body (XXVIII, 998 or 954). He does not however believe in human survival but only in the pervasive Christ-spirit

---

* See my article 'Lawrence, Joyce and Powys', *Essays in Criticism*, XI. 4 (Oct. 1961).

(XXVIII, 986-7 or 943; and see 1005 or 961). He is now willing and anxious to return to Nell. His progress shows a move from orthodoxy through mystic experience to a consummation of Wordsworthian affinities.

In contrast we have John Geard, the miracle-working mayor of Glastonbury. Sam rejects God as ' First Cause ' because of his, or its, evil; Geard tries to channel and use the good within that God to break nature's laws (XXIII 738-9 or 708-9). Sam's self-sacrifices are alien to Geard who *exploits* ' Christ ' almost as an equal and once even appears to accord a greater respect to Merlin (XXVIII, 950-1 or 909; XIX, 594 or 571). To Sam his works appear to have a devilish stamp (XVI, 491 or 474).

This prophet of a new religion, for such is his claim, is gross, ugly and untidy, and compared to such creatures, not in Powys's world to be despised, as toad and mud-turtle. He has black, demonic eyes. His religion is externally that of a crude revivalist, his favourite terms ' Blood of Christ ' or just ' the Blood ' earning him the nick-name of ' Bloody Johnny '. Another favourite of his, to which we are first introduced just when he is penetrating the secret of the Grail, is ' Bugger me black ' (XV, 471-3 or 456-7). He is strongly erotic, living from his whole, animal self. In the haunted room of Mark's Court the name of ' Nineue ', Merlin's love, comes into his mind; he dreams of it; and finally hears it clairaudiently, and by terrific psychic effort attempts to bring peace to the earth-bound ghost. His powers are titanic : he can project his consciousness ' as if it had been a stone flung from a catapult ' to the very bounds of the universe (XV, 468-9 or 453-4). He thrusts his mind like a ' lance ' into the body of a woman dying of cancer, and heals her (XXIII, 740 or 709); and he raises a child from death (XXVII, 933-5 or 893-5).

His origins are Saxon (XV, 432 or 419) and his wife is Welsh. His new religion is rather educational than devotional; in his lecture-hall we are nearer esoteric mysteries than any Church; and it is suggested that he is under some evil spell from the old Celtic magicians (XXIX, 1095 or 1046). Christ has told him that every least insect has an immortal soul (XXX, 1136-7 or 1084-5). Having gone so far, he wants death, and when the flood comes wins it through a semi-suicide motivated by ' excess of life ' (XXIX, 1090 or 1041).

Though a Saxon, Geard with his Welsh wife touches that Powysian strain of Celtic or pre-Celtic mystery that we found in Christie, whose mother was Welsh and whose book *Slate* suggested Wales, in *Wolf Solent*. This strain is now to grow stronger; it is concerned with (i) evil and (ii) some ' secret ' that can release man from evil bondage. Its main exponent in *A Glastonbury Romance* is Mr Owen Evans, a Welshman who marries Geard's daughter Cordelia. In Mr Evans the abysmal but undefined evils of Brand Renshaw and Squire Urquhart are given an appallingly precise definition. His is the root-evil of Powys's universe : sadism. It wields Cerne Giant powers.

He is a mild and academically minded man working in a book and curio shop, being a devoted scholar of old Welsh texts and at work on a life of Merlin. He is at pains to emphasise the pre-Christian lineage of the Grail. His sadistic obsession has a precise form : the desire to see a skull and vertebræ broken by a blunt instrument. He derives sexual satisfaction from telling himself stories (XVI, 518 or 500) — is there an *indirect* relation to Wolf's ' mythology '? — which constitute a kind of dramatic ' performance ' (XXIX, 1068 or 1020). This evil streams in from the negative element of the double-natured, good-and-evil, First Cause, or God. Once when Mr Evans is wondering whether Geard's white magic could help him, ' as if in mockery ' of Geard's powers

> there moved, there stirred, there awoke, in the remote circles of Being beyond this wild sky, the appalling perilous stuff in the double-natured First Cause. In its primordial Evil, as with its wavering searchlight it fathomed the numberless worlds of its living victims, the First Cause struck straight down now at the responsive nerve of Mr Evans' vice, and as it stirred that poison it gave itself up to an orgasm of egocentric contemplation.
>
> (XXV, 848 or 812)

Mr Evans then bites a turnip whereon is an infinitesimal creature at that moment ' enjoying or suffering from ' the same mania : the evil is universal. His only hope is that Christ is ' outside Nature ' (XIII, 362 or 352).

He seeks help from his Welsh studies. They seem to speak in the needed terms, whereas so much else seems, to a man who knows the abysmal nature of Evil, superficial (XXIII, 771-2 or 739-40; XIII, 362 or 352). Welsh mythology with its corpse-god (XXIV, 788 or 755) and rumours of the Grail messenger as hideous (XVI, 509 or 491-2; XXIX, 1071 or 1023), seemed to know it all. In one story Merlin tore the horns off a stag (XXIX, 1049 or 1002-3; 1077 or 1029). Mr Evans dwells on the mysterious word ' Esplumeoir ', the place, or dimension, into which Merlin disappeared (VI, 169 or 179; XXIX, 1048-9 or 1002, 1105 or 1056).

He attempts to exorcise his obsession by acting Christ in the Glastonbury Passion-Play and during the crucifixion issues of good and evil, of Christ and nature, are reviewed and deployed in fearful antagonism. The attempt failing, the century-old implement of the Crucifix, designed to thwart this very evil, gives way, following the erotic flavour of Powys's religious mysticism, to another power; the power of normal sex-attraction. Cordelia at a climax realises that her husband is in danger. He knows that a murder, provoked by Mad Bet, is being planned, and wishes to *witness* it: every stage of his temptation has been described, even to the exactitude of noting that at the moment when he is wholly dedicated to his course, sexual excitement is stilled, since the impulse is now permeating his total self (XXIX, 1051 or 1004). Now Cordelia sets her charms, poor though they are, against her husband's demoniac course. Who, Mr Evans once wondered (XXV, 831 or 796), is the true Grail Messenger, the hideous Mad Bet or the homely Cordelia? Sadism or normal sex? She strips naked to allure him, and succeeds to the extent that they hurry to the scene, though too late to prevent the crime. Mr Evans sees what he has dreamed of, and is sick. The powers are balanced.

The Grail in old Cymric is associated with a mysterious twilight (XXIX, 1052 or 1005), and Evans certainly at one point associates Mad Bet, who prompts the crime that arouses his obsession, with the Grail Messenger (XXIX, 1071 or 1023). Has this ancient wisdom power to purge a mind such as his (XXV, 837 or 801-2; 843 or 807-8; 848-9 or 812-13)? Its colour was the 'mystic' blue, and it and all its 'dark and wondrous dreams' were driven by the invaders to Wales (XXIV, 788 or 755-6). It was a wisdom in which the seeming incompatibles, the opposites, of being and not-being, life and death, were somehow in alliance (XXIII, 772 or 740). Such was the 'Living Corpse' of Uther Pendragon and in moments of fervour Mr Evans looks like a corpse (XXIV, 788 or 755; XXIII, 772 or 740; XXIX, 1068 or 1020). The union goes deeper than that union of the sexual and the anal, though it too is a life-death union, which we meet in the story of Sam and the phraseology of Geard. Though in Mr Evans's mind the 'secret' of ancient Welsh poetry was akin to 'some monstrous Rabelaisian jest' (XXV, 843 or 807-8), this is only a step towards the darker problem of death. Sam, Geard and Evans all take different, deeply Powysian, roads in which religion is saturated in erotic feeling. To Mr Evans's pre-Christian 'secret' we shall return in *Maiden Castle*.

A Glastonbury Romance has in it much else. An opposition of capitalism and communism is well presented. Though one communist leader is unpleasant another has prophetic status and the capitalist, even while he is planning to replace old Glastonbury by modern industrialisation, is given a Tolstoyan sympathy. Against such male planning the mystique of Glastonbury has the support, primarily, of women (XXIV, 778 or 746; 783 or 751). As for the people, the canvas is wide and searching. At one point a terrible female face corresponds to uttermost evil (IX, 256 or 252-3); the boy Elphin who hero-worships Sam is exquisitely drawn; rustics are as true as Hardy's; we have an interesting philosophical anarchist; Persephone is a typical Powys girl of boy-like attractiveness; and Euphemia Drew worthily exemplifies Powys's respect for old maids. The manipulation of this vast concourse of themes and persons, treated simultaneously in width and in depth, is staggering, and the realism attained remarkable. Amazing as are the events, they are all on, or near, the frontiers of possibility. The psychological and spiritual insights show a daring and a penetration in comparison with which many great classics fall to the level of escapist fiction. *A Glastonbury Romance* is less a book than a Bible.

The final Flood, strongly realised in all the horror of its unnatural mingling of elements, has been forecast from time to time during the narrative. It may be related to both the sub-world and the super-world of our various human delineations, and to the great beyond, eternity as against time; and to the cleansing of an agonised world. It is a fearful invasion of earth by sea; of life as we know it by a power non-human and sinister like the sea in *Rodmoor*, which may nevertheless yet be, like the death it symbolises, the 'primal element' and 'great maternal Womb' of all earthly existence (XXX, 1158 or 1105). But life must assert itself against death. So the Towers of Cybele, the earth-goddess, era after era, must arise, asserting human aspirations (XXX, 1172-4 or 1118-20). We are left with the enigmatic words, 'Never. Or always'. Powys's last story will be entitled '*All or Nothing*'.

In both *Wood and Stone* and *Wolf Solent* Weymouth and open sea stand for freedom and brightness; at one point everything in

Wolf's life seemed to be gravitating towards Weymouth (*Wolf Solent*, XXIV, 579 or 552). In *A Glastonbury Romance* the sea's scent impinges on ' our temporary flesh and blood ', carrying intimations across aeons of time of some pre-natal experience (XXX, 1117-8 or 1067). To Weymouth, called ' Sea-Sands ', we move in *Jobber Skald* (1935; USA, as ' *Weymouth Sands* ', 1934).

Here, in contrast to the sinister Lenty Pond and the invading flood-waters of *A Glastonbury Romance*, water and land are the happier for being clearly demarked, each in its own realm. Correspondingly, characterisation is the firmer, those psychic essences to which the sea here, rather as in Ibsen's *The Lady from the Sea*, corresponds being also more exactly placed. The effect is what we call ' realistic ' and ' objective ', and the occult, already covered by the sea, is the less obtrusive. Invigorating airs contrast with the almost enervate fecundities of *Wolf Solent*, whose weighted afternoons and sunsets, together with the giant sun-furnace of *A Glastonbury Romance*, are replaced, in exquisite descriptions, by the elixirs of dawn.

The sea is in our minds throughout. Its difference in tone from the sinister East-coast sea of *Rodmoor* marks an advance in Powys's steady assimilation of dangerous powers. Our new sea is friendly and fascinating. We are aware of its sounds and scents, its shells, rock-pools, sea-weeds, amphibious life-forms, fishes, gulls, tides, mud-banks, boats, the light-house; even, as an inn-sign, a sea-serpent. Different varieties of sand, wet and dry, are meticulously described, and so are the holiday crowds that gather on them. Human reference is continual. Sea and sea-life define human thought and deep sea the unconscious. The sea is felt to be still within us; but it is more; it is (IV, 117) infinitude.

Earth-land is occasionally remembered, but major references are comparatively few. We have our usual reminder of ancient earth-works, Arthur's Circle succeeding Leo's Hill, Poll's Camp and Glastonbury Tor, but its part in the narrative is slight. And there is the ' White ' or ' Stone ' Giant, that is the Cerne Giant, formerly a candidate for Mr Urquhart's reprehensible book but now regarded as a source of sexual and spiritual inspiration (XIV, 551-2; see V, 125, 158-9; VI, 196; X, 352; XIII, 486). Our main elemental interest, apart from the sea, is the vast rock of Shell-Back, or Portland. Sea and rock-promontory face each other as two elemental beings, like the earth and sky confrontations of *Wolf Solent*, only more solidly emphatic. The tawny and evilly impregnated Leo's Hill of *Wood and Stone* is to be contrasted with this grey-white Portland promontory; in Chapter XXVIII (699) of the earlier story it was explicitly suggested that its marbled strength might perhaps possess a power able to save one from the power of Leo's Hill. Locked weightily to earth's centre it stands against the sea as a rampart of eternal stability against unending motion (X, 359). But there is no ultimate conflict, since both equally house the supernal powers, the one eternal and the other infinite. In them these two vast imponderables are embodied. Elsewhere the 'Cyclopean embankment' of Shingle (i.e. Chesil) Beach dividing earth from 'the unresting waters' is called a master-stroke of the 'demiurgic artist' (XV, 576).

From these two elemental powers — from both of them — grows Jobber Skald, Powys's most impressive male creation and just such a man as D. H. Lawrence was always striving to create. He is of Herculean stature and massive proportions, his countenance is swarthy and his forehead 'corrugated' (as at III, 57; XIII, 493); 'saturnine' as a 'bronze sculpture' (XIII, 490) and seeming, though his ancestors came over with the Vikings (III, 58), Spanish rather than Nordic (XIII, 490). He has strong sensual qualities and is given a Lawrentian description : 'His shoulders were so broad, his hips, flanks and buttocks so thin, that his form did actually resemble a classic figure on an archaic frieze' (X, 373). Though a simple man, his personality is authoritative, even 'towering' (VI, 191-3). His parents lived on Shell-Back; he grows from it. It is part of him in a far deeper sense than that in which Leo's Hill is part of James Anderson in *Wood and Stone*. When he speaks of his 'native stone' his voice is 'reverential'; it is as though 'he had a vein of oolite in his disposition, that makes him so far-off from everybody and yet so familiar with everybody'; in suffering he becomes 'like an image of desolation carved in a darker, rougher stone than his native oolite' (X, 350; XIII, 504). But he is not only of the rock. He is also 'full of the magic of the sea'; drawing near it his nostrils 'dilated like a gigantic sea-horse, snuffing his native element'; his mood responds to the sea's; he is like a sea-god or merman (V, 171; VIII, 252-3; X, 363, 373). As 'jobber', taking on jobs of various kinds, he has his spluttering little car the *Slug* and his boat the *Cormorant*.

Though so elementally conceived, he is to be regarded less as one of Powys's many symbolical giants than as a simple study of a strong but ordinary man. By nature he is a worker with his hands rather than with his mind and not even quite in place as jobber (X, 351). He has however imagination, and is a reader. In the story he functions as champion of the labourers in the Saxon quarry on Shell-Back whose livelihood is threatened by the capitalist-brewer Dogberry Cattistock; and he carries a heavy stone as symbol and implement of retribution, with which he intends to kill his enemy. ' All Shingle Beach ', he says, ' is behind that stone ' (X, 375). He stands for simple strength and manliness against their desecration by money.

His love for Perdita Wane and hers for him, corresponding to the sea as his opposition to Cattistock corresponds to stone, is the most moving love in Powys; utterly normal, without a trace of Powysian aberration, but deep-planted, piercing each other's identity, like Heathcliff's and Cathy's in *Wuthering Heights*. Their love is symbolised by the love-union of what looks like a pair of godlike and cosmogonic human torsos among the stones of Shell-Back, such as might have been fabricated by some prehistoric race but have in fact been carved out by natural process through slow aeons of time (X, 363-5). And yet the Jobber himself is not symbolically conceived. What we are being offered is insight into the process of aeons from sea to rock and thence through nature that has created this miracle : a man. The effect would be spoiled were he more elaborately delineated; his very simplicity is his miracle. He is not mystical and does not believe in a future life. He is of creation, of time, and his favourite exclamation, with variations, from the Book of Daniel of ' a time and a time and half a time ' (II, 33, 37; X, 356; XIII, 505; XIV, 542) echoes his mystery; the mystery of time itself, of creation.

Against the Jobber's love is his murderous plan; there is separation; and the two lovers endure anguish. Here it is, described in the Jobber's marvellous words, recalling perhaps Adam Bede — the Jobber's name is Adam and his reading *Middlemarch* — but in accents of a deeper resonance :

> She thought I'd given up my oath to do for the Dog, and I never said no single word to her anent it, neither for nor against. 'Twere better I had, old friend, 'twere better I had ! For the hour came at last — a time and times and half a time, woe be to all ! — when she found out that that Shingle stone were still in my pocket, yes and in my heart, God damn and wither my soul ! in my heart, too. 'Twere a bitter moment when she found that, Bum, the bitterest I've known, and I've known many, afore and since ! There were

words between us, terrible words, my boy, words that . . . words
that . . .

(XIII, 505)

When he and Perdita are reunited a happy ending bears for once
the weight and signature of genius.

Our new prophet, Sylvanus Cobbold, is at once more easily
acceptable and more lovable than his many Powysian peers, in part
because he is already being regarded by society as half-mad and in
part because the treatment has more than Powys's usual overtone of
humour.

His appearance is extraordinary. He is tall, lean and cadaverous,
his head swaying on his long neck like a tortoise's or turtle's (XI, 395-6,
399, 405); he wears long Viking or Cymric moustaches (VII, 249), has
the digestion of a sea-lion (VIII, 258), and carries a soldier's cane. He
lives, symbolically, at the far point of Shell-Back, near the Lighthouse.
His voice is magnetic and he has a following of young girls 'whose
receptive souls' were for him 'reed-pipes through which the Absolute
played without a pause' (XIII, 497). The souls of women attune him
to the Deathless and the Immortal (VIII, 276-7).

He has various intuitions regarding death : as 'the other side of
life' (VIII, 264-5), as resembling the girl-essences he loves (VIII,
267), as a 'floating', forecast by the dancer's art, beyond life and
death as we think of them (X, 336). He defies evil, and though he is
unable to assimilate suffering into his religious beliefs, he can make
them assimilate 'the Gross, the Repulsive, the Disgusting' (XI, 395).
In addressing the Absolute he calls himself 'Caput-Anus' and
apostrophises a rope :

> Rope, rope, hang Sylvanus!
> From caput to anus
> His doings profane us,
> Rope, rope, hang Sylvanus!

(XI, 405)

Both he and his Absolute have strong sensual qualities, yet when he
sleeps with a girl he enjoys, through an assertion such as that attributed
to 'the Lamas of Thibet' of 'mind over instinct' deliberately curtail-
ing the 'great erotic force' behind creation, a 'prolongation' rather
than a 'culmination' of erotic ecstasy (XI, 393, 395). At morning he
greets sun, sea and sky with ritualistic observances and speaks a
liturgy to his garden instruments. A dancing sunbeam, whom he calls
'Trivia', causes him exquisite delight (XI, 405).

Much of Powys's developing wisdom is in Sylvanus, who, it is suggested, behaves exactly as the Absolute itself ' *should* go to work ', if it ' broke out ' (X, 342). When he asked the Absolute if it was the ' First Cause ' it replied

> that It was not the First Cause, or the Last Cause, or any other Cause ! It simply was Everything, and there was no room in Everything for the idea of Cause. There was only All there was; and it was the inherent nature, throughout eternity, for All there was to change.
>
> (XI, 428)

This is the direction Powys's thought is to take, being impelled away from the grim semi-demonic and paradoxical First Cause of *A Glastonbury Romance*. Not that Sylvanus solves the problem of evil, though he can master disgusts. When he is in the asylum he dispels the psychiatrist's theories of the unconscious as a mystery susceptible only of indirect definition by demonstrating that it can be consciously known, and before long the practitioner, who quickly wilts before him, is himself being ' practised on ' (XIV, 528). The doctor is also a vivisectionist, and though denunciations of vivisection are here cauterising, he is, as are nearly all Powys's main persons as persons, given a certain sympathy. His effeminacy arouses in Sylvanus, who is explicitly said to be *strangely* normal for a prophet, a strong defence of sexual differentiation; that is, of sexual normality (XIV, 551).

Dog Cattistock is, like his predecessor Mortimer Romer in *Wood and Stone*, honourably treated. He alone, the capitalist, is in our society the effective man of action, and by a typical stroke of Powysian irony it is he, and not the Jobber, who plunges into a stormy sea, partly it is true for propaganda, to rescue what appears to be a drowning body (VIII, 290-3). He despises the human race, and the power he best loves is power ' in suspension ' or ' in reserve ', not practised or even generally known; and the extent of his wealth remains unrevealed (XII, 457-9). That he should carry off the girl loved by our Powys-hero, Magnus Muir, is perfectly reasonable.

Magnus, with his stick, aware of his father's presence and ineffectual as a lover, conforms to type. More interesting is the half-crazy lad, Larry Zed, whose vivid boy-hood outrivals that of Lobby Torp in *Wolf Solent* or Elphin Cantle in *A Glastonbury Romance*. He is a ' queer lad ' of ' wild-animal movements ' :

She liked everything about him. She liked his green eyes. She liked his blood-red hair, with a matted elf-lock hanging loose over his forehead. She liked his white gleaming teeth. She liked his long bare forearms, as free from hairs as were her own. She liked his brown knees beneath his ragged knickerbockers. She liked his supple waist and his thin slouching body.

(V, 163)

At first devoted to his dream 'Nothing-Girl' (V, 126) he comes to experience amatory feeling of fiery strength, his personal drama inter-threading the main narrative. He has a wild beauty. We see 'his green eyes shining with the phosphorus of anger', and when thwarted he stands 'stunned, taut and trembling, his eyes full of angry tears' (XI, 386, 389). He has sweetness of temperament and a native chivalry. He endures his little tragedy, adjusting himself 'to that renunciation that is as ancient as our troubled race' (XIV, 538).

Besides these, are Sylvanus's brother Jerry, the famous clown, and his wife Lucinda, a woman of mysterious Clytemnestra-like evil; Gipsy May and her swift, furtive movements and Tarot cards; Sippy Ballard, the obtrusive and self-confident clerk in his honking car; and the philosophic Richard Gaul, who when asked by a girl if her ecstatic pleasure in the 'glittering bodies' of youthful bathers is wrong, replies:

What you represent at present is the third rung of the philosophic ladder to the Contemplative Ecstasy. When you have reached the ninth rung you will find — you will lose — I mean you will gain —

(XIII, 489)

In which centuries of idealism stand exquisitely transfixed.

Despite the vivisectional nightmare, *Jobber Skald* is a happy book. Sun, sea, and grey-white (V, 158-9) Shell-Back stone dominate as spiritual presences, as part of a dream-fabric, yet close and real:

But Shell-Back, as it lay before them, rising tier by tier over its terraces of old walls and grey roofs, seemed to be tugging at its tether in that luminous and liquid haze, seemed to be straining at this gigantic rope of transparent stones, agates and cornelians, which bound it to the mainland. The huge lime-stone rock seemed to have no roots, under this enchanted light, in any solid earth. It seemed to be riding, just as the battleships in the harbour seemed to be riding, upon a liquid abyss of opalescent water that sank down to the antipodes. And the Jobber got the impression that this stupendous mass of oolite was really afloat today in this translucent calm; not only afloat, but longing to drift off, to sail out and away, over the surface of that halcyon sea.

(X, 350)

Sylvanus too, the morning sea-breeze fresh and cool, feels that the whole promontory is being lifted up as if 'Nature were returning to God', the Relative to the Absolute, 'Life to some mysterious Beyond-Life' (XI, 402). For him sunlight and water together — Wolf remembered seeing them at Weymouth during his Saturnian revelation — were 'the nearest revelation of Ultimate Being' attainable by man (XI, 406). Colours are sharp and clean. At midday the sky's 'blue intensity' is fringed 'by a delicate film of Chinese-white' on the horizon (XIII, 496). At sunset the sky is like a 'piece of unbroken gold-leaf' as the sun draws 'a motionless golden path across the dark-blue water', the blue and gold suggesting some religious ritual (X, 363). 'Enchantment' and 'enchanted' are here natural words. The key-tone is that of dawn. The great dawn near the conclusion is less gold than our dominating white, the colour of the White Giant and of grey-white Shell-Back, recalling the mystic whiteness in *Rodmoor*:

> Minutes and minutes flowed over them, and the link between them became like another dawn, whiter, ghostlier, more inscrutable still, mounting up through a yet deeper dark. Then came a time when the whole wide stretch of waters threw open its tremulous dawn-porches to their intense gaze. Grey, and yet not grey, metal-livid rather, like the dumb glimmer of ten thousand sword-blades, the sea unrolled its leagues of shivering expanse. It grew whiter and ever whiter, and its whiteness was not the whiteness of death, nor yet the whiteness of light or of life. It was the whiteness of the spirit. It was the whiteness of that mysterious act of creation that came even before the word.

(XIV, 538)

Very rarely does Powys use the word 'spirit'. This book contains one of Powys's few full-length descriptions of music, here compared to a sea of 'liquid ether' like 'mother-of-pearl' (VII, 213). If *Jobber Skald* has comparatively few references to the occult, that is because the spirit-powers are here housed in an empearled creation. It is Powys's most consummate work of embodied mysticism.

POSTSCRIPT ON WEYMOUTH SANDS (February 1964)

Jobber Skald has now been reissued by Messrs. Macdonald & Co. under its first, American, 1934, title *Weymouth Sands*. The original text is followed, and the actual place-names now appear instead of the fictional names used in the 1935 English edition as a cautionary measure, as described by Mr E. R. H. Harvey in his valuable preface to the new edition. Sea-Sands is again Weymouth; Shell-Back, Portland; Shingle Beach, Chesil Beach; Peat Bog, Lodmoor; Arthur's Circle, Maiden Castle; and so on. With the help of the one-inch Ordnance Survey Map (published by the Ordnance Survey, Chessington, Surrey) the people's movements can now be easily followed.

One of Powys's 1935 alterations had a certain validity. In *Jobber Skald,* ' the White Horse ' of *Weymouth Sands,* a figure cut on a hill near Weymouth, is changed throughout to ' the White Giant ' or ' the Stone Giant '. Powys seems to have seized the opportunity to imagine the presence of his well-loved Cerne Giant, though he is of chalk rather than of stone, where there had originally been no room for him; for he exists some distance from Weymouth. The nature of the change, which Powys no doubt enjoyed, may be seen from the alteration of ' as when the great White Horse was cut for Victoria's grandfather ' in the 1934 and 1963 editions (1963; V, 163) to ' as when the great White Giant was cut for the men of antiquity ' in the edition of 1935 (V, 159).

To help the reader of the new edition to follow my own page references I give the page numerals of the chapter openings in *Jobber Skald*: I, 1; II, 27; III, 49; IV, 86; V, 125; VI, 173; VII, 208; VIII, 251; IX, 296; X, 326; XI, 379; XII, 433; XIII, 473; XIV, 523; XV, 557. From these the position of any one reference may be roughly calculated.

Ancient history has been with us in Leo's Hill, Poll's Camp, Glastonbury Tor, and Arthur's Circle; and the hill-giant of Cerne Abbas. An ancient mound is now to be our central concern in *Maiden Castle* (1937), written around the prehistoric earth-work near Dorchester dating back beyond Christian and Roman times to a Celtic or pre-Celtic past. Leo's Hill in *Wood and Stone* radiated pagan evil powers; now, within Powys's progress, similar powers are to be searched, but in expectance of a potential good. *Maiden Castle* is a transition work. On it pivots Powys's shift of interest from Wessex to Wales.

Our new story is intellectualised and interpretative. The Powys-hero's unconventional and sterile love-making is deliberately reflected in his name, Dud No-man. He converses with his dead mother and has for ten years made nightly love to his own dead wife who in the body had meant little to him. He arranges for a sum of money to take the girl Wizzie Ravelton, an elder successor to the child Dolores in *Wood and*

Stone, from a circus where she is unhappy, and he then lives with her, making love, like other Powys-heroes, and Sylvanus too, in Sylvanus's cerebral Thibetan fashion. Motherhood he believes in, but the act of paternity is repellent and he would have preferred partheno-genesis (IV, 162). When, like Wolf and Magnus, he is to lose his girl, he is denounced by her as being ' not a man ' (IX, 428). Like the others, he is in Wordsworthian contact with a secret beside which normal love pales (VIII, 353), and it is this semi-mystical quality which renders his love approaches themselves less sterile than they seem :

> It meant nothing to her that there was in this a proof of the intensity of his feeling, a proof of its etherealised sensuality, of its all-pervasiveness and absorbing diffusion.
>
> (IX, 473)

He is writing an historical novel, which he composes by inspiration, almost in trance (III, 100-1). He responds to the past. He is our extreme development and clearest exposition of the ' Powys-hero '. Despite his apparent ineffectuality, his stick is significantly called a ' Cerne Giant ' stick (VI, 225; VII, 275; IX, 429).

Wizzie is Powys's greatest success in full-length female characterisa-tion. In female psychology he is always expert and his realisation of girls in mutual relationship particularly good, but his girls are created so peculiarly from ' within ' that we have the less sense of them as objectively differentiated persons. Many of them are, as it were, the same, normal girl, whereas his males tend to be brilliantly character-ised eccentrics. His most vivid girls as units have been those who have, or touch, boy-like attributes, such as Gladys in *Wood and Stone,* Philippa in *Rodmoor,* and Persephone Spear in *A Glastonbury Romance;* or who have esoteric extensions, like Gerda and Christie. Gladys and Philippa were simultaneously attractive and cruel; in them the bisexual was, or seemed to be, distrusted. Now, within the unfurling process of Powys's assimilative expansions, we have in Wizzie a complete and lovable feminine study the firmer for its bisexual pointing.

She has been brought up in a Convent and in the Circus. At first pathetic, she grows to a passionate strength, and is capable of a dark fury. Bought by Dud No-man, she is called a Stone or Bronze Age captive (II, 91; VII, 305), and after a while she prefers the dark and fearsome sage, Uryen Quirm, to her novelist-lover. When she wears trousers like a boy she exerts a vivid fascination (VIII, 329-52). We never forget that she is a circus-girl. She lovingly remembers her old horse, and dreams of returning to circus life, leaping in ' sky-blue ' tights ' like a shooting star ' through a ' rainbow-circle of dazzlement and wild applause '; riding on her horse's ' strong back ' through ' all the starry hoops of the world ' in a ' starry rush through the air ' (VII, 305-6; VIII, 349-50). Her quality as simple circus-girl flowers to a semi-transcendental splendour. She has the native poetry of Larry Zed.

The less attractive Thuella, an obvious descendant of Philippa and Gladys, is an artist with a ' frail androgynous being ' (I, 50), and her father Teucer Wye is an effeminate and dandified Platonist (I, 53-4; III, 131) who nevertheless has to repudiate the master when his other daughter is in danger of carrying the Platonic doctrine too far. We are in an intellectual and analytic society. Despite Powys's Platonic affinities Platonism was distrusted by Wolf and Christie and is here definitely deflated. The Roman-like and practical Mr Cask, called ' Claudius ', is an ascetic philanthropist believing in organised progress and Communism and Teucer Wye's son a Fascist claiming that his movement channels forces in youth that demand expression. Money is represented by a publisher.

Despite the narrative's academic concentrations, town-life is not important: we are little aware of Dorchester as a town. Nature is earth-nature, but it has nothing of the atmospheric quality of *Wolf Solent* or the mystical extensions of *A Glastonbury Romance*. Rather we are *on* earth as a hard, turfy, *surface*, under bright light accompanied by glittering insects and lark-music. Yellow is an emphatic colour. We have one of Powys's few fires; there was one before the final dawn of *Jobber Skald;* this one is a bon-fire on Maiden Castle, recalling the fire on Leo's Hill (*Wood and Stone*, XV, 374). *Maiden Castle* is, in its way, a fiery book made mainly from the fire of intellect as against soil, sun, sea and instinct. There is a pond, but it has no such sinister magic as Lenty Pond. There are dark abysms here, but they are abysms of the mind or of the past or abysms deep *below* earth. Their representations are Maiden, or Mai-dun, Castle itself, seat once of a nobler civilisation than ours (V, 218; VI, 227), and its interpreter, Uryen Quirm. Through these earth's flatness and opacity is felt as a covering to some hidden secret. Ancient, prehistoric, idols are unearthed, from below.

In *Wood and Stone* we met an evil old circus-man of ' corpse-like ' appearance and a face of hideous immobility (XXV, 655; 661-2). This evil is carried over into positive significance in our new sage, Uryen Quirm. He is also a composite of essences from Hastings in *Ducdame* and from Geard and the occasionally corpse-like Mr Evans in *A Glastonbury Romance*; and through him we are to attack those mysteries of evil and death which Sylvanus Cobbold could not solve. His Biblical name ' Enoch ' he has changed to ' Uryen ', the name of a prince in Welsh mythology (*A Glastonbury Romance*, XXIV, 788 or 755), of whom he thinks himself a reincarnation. He is of Welsh origin and turns out, by a symbolism of general import, to be Dud's father. Whether he is humanly convincing may be questioned, but he is best approached as a philosophical, or symbolical, creation, rather than as a man.

He is massive and giant-like and his appearance is variously associated with a corpse, metallic sculpture, solidified mist, deep water, the ocean; his face is swarthy, his hair like moss, and his eyes lifeless. He is old. Like Mr Evans, he is learned; and he can concoct mysterious medicines. Substantial though he seems he is made of ' mental stuff ' (IV, 160), and is searching, like Mr Evans, for a secret housed in ancient Welsh wisdom concerned with horror and death. To him the symbol of ' a three-horned bull with two human torsos impaled on its horns and another one transfixed on its up-curving tail ' goes ' deeper into life than anything in Plato ' (IV, 155). Mr Evans would have agreed; like Mr Evans's, Uryen's soul is ' sodden with some abominable suffering ' (IV, 157). But Uryen *is* what he thinks of. He actually exudes a deathly odour and is like a corpse-god from Welsh mythology (IV, 163; VI, 241; IV, 154; see p. 40). Because he contains these dark mysteries he is simultaneously repellent and a figure of imposing ' majesty ' (IV, 159). When he visits Maiden Castle a ghostly wind is aroused, making a weird music, rising and falling (IV, 146-54; VI, 243-4), which is Powys's theme-song for ancient Wales, to be used again in *Owen Glendower*.

Dud No-man had inherited a grotesque idol. This he associated with Spenser's ' Questing Beast ', which may, we are told, be in turn linked, through ' a gnomic allusion of Taliessin's ', with the word ' Dor-Marth ', meaning the Door of Death (III, 102-3). He is to this extent imaginatively prepared when his new-found father Uryen wills to initiate him into the Welsh secrets.

Uryen's philosophy is original. He thinks, by a striking development of Wolf Solent's sense of dangerous fascination when in the presence of such emotions (p. 33), that he can draw power from using a girl's love for another girl (IV, 166; IX, 454, 483). He emphasises the spiritual magic to be won through 'sterile passion'. This, he says, opens out the way to the 'life behind life', for everything exists in the mind and even Maiden Castle and 'all its bright grass' is really afloat on 'the dark under-sea' of human perception (VI, 236-8). Uryen's thoughts can be frightening. He claims to stand for, and even to be, a Power that is older than the sunshine because it has 'Death in it as well as life':

> It's this Power — the Power that works in me, lad, the Power that I *am* — that beats in its pain against the wall of the world.
>
> (VI, 239)

And this power arises from self-violated sex:

> Don't you see what force there is in sterile love? Why, my dear boy, it's the strongest force there is! Rampant desire unfulfilled — why, there's nothing it can't do. Stir up sex *till it would put out the sun* and then keep it sterile! That's the trick. That's the grand trick of all spiritual life.
>
> (VI, 240)

His inhuman sun-blighting and sex-blasting thoughts, arising from Powys's will to grapple with evil and death, are accompanied by a typically Powysian counter-stroke. As the sun blazes down and a lark sings Uryen interrupts his sepulchral metaphysic to 'cast an almost savage glance towards the sky as if the sun were deliberately pelting him with lark-music' (VI, 239). Later, when a bonfire is lit on *Maiden Castle* under the midday sun, the flames take on a 'supernatural' redness (VIII, 369), the conception covering the ambiguous authority, danger and transcendency together, of the mental powers as against nature and the cosmos:

> The tremendous force of the midsummer sun, for it must have been at least one o'clock by this time, seemed to be sucking up, as if with a gigantic tongue, all the life, all the vitality, all the character from those dying flames. If they were red before, they were a mockery of redness now. Some of them, in fact, as they rose into a momentary flare from the fiery heap, took to themselves the colour of fading crocuses. Others became pallid as summer lightning. One or two, just because this blazing sun and this burning metallic sky had sucked all the devilry out of them, and all the piracy, and all the life-lust, became spiritualized and etherealized,

became like candle-flames, those purest of all forms of fire, those guileless sisterhoods of fire.

(VIII, 371)

Gathered round the fire the exponents of our different philosophies feel 'something momentous' in its extinction beneath 'this majesty of burning light'.

And yet we cannot deny the power of Uryen's attempt to revive 'the old magic of the mind, the secret of which has been so often lost' until 'the Welsh, alone among the races, *hid* it instead of squandering it' (VI, 240).

Uryen opposes his son's scepticism by asserting that the supernatural is 'like the other side of the moon'; but he cannot directly answer his son's demand for a 'Yes' or 'No' regarding human survival. While admitting that the spirit-powers cannot have for him quite the reality of day-to-day existence and objects, he claims that they have that '*atmosphere of reality*' which girls understand so much better than men (VI, 221-3). Even so, *Maiden Castle* is throughout saturated in spiritualistic reference and even phenomena, as when No-man's dead wife seems actually to have written her name on a paper (VIII, 382; IX, 405; 430). Uryen himself functions as a medium for the spirits of *Maiden Castle* when he awakens the ghost-wind (VI, 244). Spirit-feeling can on occasion activate nature in the manner of *Jobber Skald*, as when No-man, climbing the hill with his father, seems to float, experiencing sensations of 'airiness and lightness' and a mysterious fragrance (VI, 225), while Maiden Castle itself becomes 'like some pearl-green convolution of an airy world-shell floating in space' (VI, 228).

Like Merlin in *Porius*, Uryen presses his head onto the earth (VI, 225). He does not look to sun and sky; these are enemies; he feels that the secret is embedded *below*, like the relics excavated from Maiden Castle (VIII, 322, 355-9), and 'that the Power of the Underworld that our old Bards worshipped, *though it was always defeated*, is the Power of the Golden Age'. That, we are told, was an age without cruelty; and one day again the power will break through, as was intended (IX, 455-6). Later, in *Morwyn*, we shall visit those depths wherein the Golden Age is sleeping.

These words are spoken when Uryen is dying. His dead eyes now flash. He claims to be himself the subject of Taliessin's prophecies, holding the inmost secret of his race, ' that straining, that longing, that yearning, that craving, that madness to break through '; it is ' Desire, but not ordinary Desire ', utterly unconventional and unsocial (IX, 455). The Power of the Golden Age, which built Maiden Castle and Stonehenge, is the same Power that ' rushes through ' him when he visits Maiden Castle. This power we have wrongly called demonic :

> It strides from world to world creating new things out of nothing! It takes Nature between its fingers and Evolution in the palm of its hand. It's more than desire. It's all the defeated longing, all the baffled longing, all the forbidden longing, all the beating against the walls, that makes the wind howl and the rain cry! And it will break through. I tell you girls this, as I've told it to Nance and as I've told it to my son. It'll break through. And when it breaks through, these four thousand years wherein the world has been deceived and has left the way will be redeemed, and what was intended to happen will be allowed to happen, and the superstition of science will be exploded forever!

(IX, 456)

His features begin to decompose. He gropes with his hands, like a beast on his hind legs; he seems to be pawing the ground; he becomes an animal, crawling on all fours. Finally ' he sank down with a weight that seemed almost superhuman, as if his form were responding to the gravitational pull of the earth's centre with a more than normal response, and lay motionless with closed eyes ' (IX, 460).

In Uryen we have Powys's attempt to personify a wisdom or wise-being which is death as well as life; animal and the inanimate as well as man; a, or the, creative principle, wronged by four thousand years of misguided progress. *Maiden Castle,* except for Wizzie — and the child Lovie — must be read for its philosophy. It is a hinge and a precursor. Though his conflict with the sun denotes a limitation, we can nevertheless say that in Uryen much of Powys's future speculation lies curled as in a womb. In terms of this extraordinary and half-repellent personality Powys is forcing a passage towards his Golden Age.

CHAPTER IV
Philosophy and Autobiography

Powys's more explicit philosophy during this period is covered by four books published in the thirties: *The Meaning of Culture* (1930), *In Defence of Sensuality* (1930), *A Philosophy of Solitude* (1933), and *The Art of Happiness* (1935). The first is a comparatively impersonal survey of cultural engagements. The second contains one of Powys's clearest definitions of his central doctrine :

> What this psychic-sensuous ecstasy that I am defending really implies is a *direct embrace of life*. It is, in fact, a sublimated synthesis of the sex-instinct, the hunger-instinct, the thirst-instinct. It is a see-hear-touch-taste-smell complex, with an overtone of psychic imagination. It corresponds in human beings to the enjoyment-feeling of trees, animals, birds, fishes, and reptiles.
>
> (V, 169)

The experience, he says, touches dimensions beyond those recognised by science. Apart from any such ' dimensions ', since all the senses are involved (see *Mortal Strife*, IX, 148), we may suppose it more rich than any known to our one-by-one perceptions. Other implications are developed in *A Philosophy of Solitude,* which worries more explicitly at the relation of mind to matter. Consciousness adheres to ' some nucleus of magnetic energy ' which is connected with, yet different from, the body (II, 46, 55). The solitary ' I ' creates a ' thought-body ' or ' etheric mask ' (II, 55; III, 83), able to make the elemental contacts (II, 54). The inanimate holds a secret revelation not to be had from animals or even plants, and to penetrate it loneliness is necessary (II, 67; V, 172; III, 92). Wordsworth was fond of solitary persons (I, 38). Much of our unhappiness comes from living in crowds and groups in contrast to the peaceful and lonely families of the lost ' Golden Age ' (VI, 184).

The analysis of mental projection is carried further in *The Art of Happiness,* wherein Powys counsels what he calls an ' Ichthian act ' of the mind, making the spirit leap beyond normal existence into the unknown dimension beyond life and death (I, 23-31; II, 84); also ' an act of de-carnation ', separating, or seeming to separate, soul and

56

body, but aiming no further (I, 25; II, 84); and a third, 'the Panergic act', grasping with concentrated will on simple elemental pleasures (I, 62, 68; II, 84-5; IV, 155).

Happiness can be won by the simplest acts of contemplation. Anything touched by the sun is miraculous:

> Thus transfigured, the mere fact of the thing resting there, in its immobility, with the immense gulfs of air sinking away into illimitable space behind it, evokes, as it lies back upon the calm mystery of dawn or of evening, the feeling that it is the golden threshold of some land of enchantment into which our soul can enter and find a solution of all the paradoxes of life.
>
> (V, 188)

It should not be difficult, especially for a generation brought up on what is called 'symbolist' poetry, to see that what Powys is announcing is really the gospel of poetry itself, and of painting too, ably discussed in *The Meaning of Culture* and the essay on El Greco in *Visions and Revisions,* wherein the poet or painter enjoys and makes others enjoy a supreme satisfaction from just such insights as these.

The *Autobiography* (1934), driving deeper and ranging wider than the earlier and comparatively indecisive attempt at self-revelation in the *Confessions of Two Brothers* (USA, 1916), is a study not of a writer but of a personality. During the years covered by it he was a professional lecturer on literature, first in England and afterwards in America. His audiences were varied, but were, it seems, predominantly female; he certainly appears to have aroused a peculiarly deep response in women. His technique was as much an actor's as a lecturer's, a free use of gesture, mime, and on occasion an almost ecstatic action being employed in the making of what he calls his 'dithyrambic' analyses. He was, in fact, *living* literature. Words and actions came unprepared; it was all highly inspirational. These performances constitute a fascinating and perhaps unique example of a man acting the greatest literatures of the world, including many strains too from Oriental religion, in his own person; and quite apart from the lectures, the story told in the *Autobiography* reveals a personality in which those great literatures and religions appear to have attained a more comprehensive self-consciousness than in any other on record.

Such a man inevitably stands in contrast to those externals of respectability and culture on which the greatest literature, by the very nature of its profundity, constitutes an attack. Powys's supporters, and they are also those he most wishes to affect, are those in psychological troubles; and repressed minorities such as — in so far as they are oppressed rather than in power — Catholics, Communists and Jews. From Catholics he received a deep and true understanding (VIII, 323); he likes nuns and reverences those ' sensitive Beings ', Old Maids (X, 520-1); and the American negroes aroused not only his sympathy but almost his adoration (X, 507-8). His sympathy for all pariah types is no simple matter of impersonal benevolence, for he regards himself as abnormal and is at pains to persuade us of his psychological aberrations. He is willing to be regarded as a charlatan with the implied corollary that any genuine contact with the greater powers must today be regarded as charlatanism. Throughout runs a strong comoedic insistence; often he sees himself as a clown (X, 537-8).

His inner life shows a coming together of sexuality and religion : he is always striving towards a harmonisation of these great powers. The link is necessarily nature, the ground on which they meet, and Powys is a nature-worshipper. Like his ' great master ' (VII, 275) Wordsworth, he has experiences of nature-mysticism, sensing the life of the supposedly inanimate. He is however more particularly moved by places where nature is blended with a human past such as old paths and barns, or stone buildings worn by weather and covered by lichens and moss. In these experiences sensual enjoyment is one with eternal insight (VII, 289, 291; VIII, 330, 378-9; IX, 434-6; X, 517).

Wordsworth too liked a human reference and for him the past events that rendered localities numinous were often, indeed usually, macabre.* Now Powys is also, though rather differently, fascinated by the macabre, and he admits that sadism has been in him a recurring obsession. Sadistic actions have been few, and only in youth, but the corresponding *ideas,* especially as stimulated by certain books, persisted. By nature and also in part by reaction from the horror, Powys has been abnormally kind, doing his best in a number of ways to ease the paths of his human enemies, of animals, and even insects.

We may perhaps, with Wordsworth's love of macabre localities as a fusing medium, attempt to establish a relationship between Powys's nature mysticism and the sadistic obsession. Here and elsewhere he makes it clear that almost any external object may be mystically apprehended, including such as are of human fabrication. Both experiences, the mystical and the sadistic, may accordingly be

---

* These I have discussed in *The Starlit Dome,* I.

regarded as unions of the ego with an opposite; either externally with the objective universe or internally by the enjoyment of fantasies the opposite, and this may be true even if the fantasies are not of the sadistic kind, of the subject's normal psychological structure. If an obsession is sadistic ' nature ' is very clearly involved, since sadism is a reflection within human sexuality of the negative blood-law implanted in the universe. But Powys claims in late middle-age to have mastered these fantasies, for he regards them as containing a telepathic potential of evil influence (I, 10-11; IV, 121; V, 191). He carefully avoids any sadistic glamour in his work (I, 8-9).

Ordinary sexual intercourse receives little or no emphasis. Sex is strong but abnormal, and it is abnormal because it is half spiritualised and aiming rather at consciousness and diffusion than at a physically located action. Sex-play, we are told, tends to avoid, as does Sylvanus Cobbold, consummation in order to receive a ' Golden Age,' diffused experience (VIII, 364-5, 379). Powys's ' inner life-flame ' withdraws ' with a shrinking of its whole nature from contact with ordinary, normal, natural sex-expression ' (VI, 207; and see VII, 275). And yet he is sex-dominated. The very word ' girl ' electrifies his imagination (VI, 205; VIII, 358), and for long periods he was obsessed by ' frenzied eye-lust ' for certain aspects of girlish figures and limbs, though he could never admire the whole female form (VI, 242-3). His best glimpses were gained on beaches or under stage conditions in variety shows. What he was searching out was ' a pleasure that was sexual and yet not sexual, that had to do with women, and yet had not the faintest connection with women ' (VI, 244). Much of his inner life was devoted to this ' sylphic ' (VI, 205, and throughout) quest.

The visionary ' lust ' is called ' impersonal ' and ' anonymous ' (VI, 207; VII, 299, 307; VIII, 379). Actual girls, as distinguished from the visions caught from them, tended to falsify expectance, and the male sex appears to have stood the test better. Once he wonders if women are better representatives of the sylphic than certain men (VI, 206). He certainly shows an electric response, from school-days onwards, to male beauty (e.g. III, 107; IV, 114-5, 138-9; V, 197; VI, 207, 221; X, 442). Since he denies a specifically homosexual impulse (IX, 426) we may call the response aesthetic. He once writes of himself as ' a *sort* of Homosexual, not physically but mentally — or even shall we hazard that tricky word — spiritually ' (*Letters to Louis Wilkinson;* 17 August, 1948; 252). Boys seem to have been impressed on his visual *memory* more clearly than girls (VI, 215). At Cambridge he found that his darker fantasies were quiescent (V, 167-8; 191). For one of these seraphic* illuminations he uses the terms ' elf ' and ' Ariel ' (VI, 207), recalling the boys named ' Elphin ' in *A Glastonbury Romance* and *Owen Glendower* and Larry Zed with his ' elf-lock ' in *Jobber Skald*. Louis Wilkinson is regularly referred to by the designation given him by T. F. Powys as ' the Archangel.' Llewelyn was as beautiful as an ' angel ', and said to recall the half-feminine beauty of the Fair Youth in Shakespeare's Sonnets (VIII, 347). On meeting Powys's son a stranger compared him to a ' Greek god ' (VI, 233). The novels provide numerous analogies.

The girls arouse what Powys regularly calls an *impersonal* lust, though the word ' lust ' scarcely holds for him the usual connotations; whereas male youth appeals more to the mind. Each exists near the border-line of sex-impulse and religious, or metaphysical, vision. Perhaps what Powys wants is what he calls some ' Saturnian ' sex different ' from the masculine and feminine that we know '; this, whatever it be, remains his ' religion ' and ' beatific vision ' (VI, 206-7). We may call it a ' bisexual ' or ' seraphic ' intuition. Though Platonism can be slighted in *Wolf Solent* and *Maiden Castle,* references to Socrates, Plato and Eros are here freely sprinkled, as when we hear of ' the Platonic idea of slender sylphid forms ' with ' little oval heads, and hips like those of delicate boys ' (X, 472). The girls that moved him in variety shows were sometimes dressed, as he once tried to dress a girl friend, like ' those enchanting boy-girls or girl-boys ' in Shakespeare (VI, 241; X, 486). In such ways Powys is realising a unification of mind and sexual instinct. It is a way of self-realisation through self-reflection, since he himself, though physically strong and powerful, yet recognises in himself strong feminine affinities, using again and again such terms for himself as ' girlish ' or ' womanish '. He enjoys imagining himself a girl in love (VII, 274-5) and asserts that the power possessed by Dostoievsky and Shakespeare of temporarily becoming women was his when the spirit of the Druids or Taliessin possessed him (X, 528). The Druidic reference is apt, since one of his life-long aims was to become a magician (VIII, 352, 357).

Powys's sadistic instincts, he tells us, were of female quality (IX, 426). We may compare the darkly evil women in the novels

---

* ' Seraphic ' is my own term, as used for my discussions throughout *The Golden Labyrinth* and in the Epilogue to the 1962 reissue of *The Christian Renaissance.*

(pp. 40-1, 47, 65-6, 69-70, 99-100). These women are vaguely delineated, but so are all his women as ' characters ', unless touching the bisexual, not because they are less interesting to him, but because they are so near. We can perhaps hazard this four-fold pattern. His male and Apollonian tendencies are attracted by male youth within a mental world which subscribes to ethic and gentleness, since Powys's normal behaviour witnesses an extreme of self-sacrifice, and even masochism. His Aphrodisiac and Dionysian tendencies respond to girls as sylphs and *at an extreme* to the sadistic. Though this last grouping seems strange, yet in the novels Christie in *Wolf Solent*, Morwyn in *Morwyn* and Tegolin in *Owen Glendower,* all directly or by association support it (pp. 31-2, 65-6, 69). Girls are close to nature, to both its good and its evil. Wordsworth's girls were ' elementals ', wild nature and girl-hood being somehow ' bound up together ' (VII, 275; VIII, 334; IX, 414). My present analysis is no longer thinking in terms of opposites : we are supposing the male element in the psyche to respond to male and the female to female; it is a kind of bisexual homosexuality, like to like, in four-fold pattern. Powys once sees himself as a ' sylph ' or ' salamander ' contemplating the limbs of a ' sylph ' or ' undine ' (VII, 275-6).

The heart of the *Autobiography* is Powys's account of his association in Italy with a lady of intellect and artistic perception who dressed as a boy. The ' ambiguous beauty of our boy-girl ' (IX, 410) endowed him temporarily with a sense of ' supernatural ' or ' spiritual ' power; he was, he says, in that very state which ' I had been obscurely fumbling my way towards through all my lusts and my obsessions ' (IX, 408-9). This is our perfect key, opening through the bisexual adoration to supernal power. The association, which had the joint qualities of female fascination and male companionship, endured for days on this level : the seraphic was, temporarily, incarnate.

Despite the higher experiences, there remained always, or nearly always, the recurring sadistic obsession, together with a tendency, such as Adrian Sorio in *Rodmoor* also experienced, to imagine when in the presence of human excellence, with a Rabelaisian refusal to forget its extensions into foulness, some hideous accompaniment and desecration (IX, 410).

The personality recorded in the *Autobiography* and witnessed by accounts of Powys's lecturing and by his own creative writing may be defined as a unique summation of Western literature together with various strains, for references to these are frequent, of Oriental religion. By both natural instinct and deliberate purpose he embodies that far reach of the Western imagination covered by Prospero and Ariel in Shakespeare's *The Tempest*. Like Shakespeare's Glendower, precursor of Prospero, he has, or imagines that he has, at his disposal, ' trillions ' of spirits ' from the vasty deep ' (XII, 630; *1 Henry IV*, III. i. 53), sending out his healing thoughts as ' coloured angels ' (VIII, 373; XII, 630-2, 638-41); or invoking the souls of dead Indians to help Llewelyn (XII, 635). Though he prays, as did Sylvanus Cobbold, to various elemental and other deities, his spiritual efforts for men and animals are less like prayers than commands to a power or powers under his own control (XII, 632, 639), his relation to them corresponding to Prospero's mastery of Ariel. His identification with the elements is such that he has actually himself experienced the Ariel sensations of floating in air or flaming as fire, and of astral-travelling about the globe (VII, 276; IX, 409). Spirit-healing such as Powys's, which must be distinguished from ' faith-healing ', is a well-known and widespread practice. When attacking the uselessness of vivisection Powys observes that while this unavailing horror persists people all over the world are being healed by spiritual methods (XII, 640). There is however a reverse side to Powys's powers. Those who have incurred his anger have so invariably suffered misfortune that he has, as it were, been *forced* into a life of almost neurotic benevolence (VIII, 352; IX, 408-9; X, 516; and see VIII, 338-9). Powys's early ambition to become a magician was no idle dream.

When late in life he turned seriously to writing, he deliberately reduced his psychic practices in order to preserve his powers for the other medium (XII, 641), rather as Uryen Quirm in *Maiden Castle* (IX, 456) found his psychic powers leaving him when he turned to writing. Powys regards his books as propaganda for his *tao* or life-way; but not quite propaganda in the ordinary sense, since he asserts that his visionary narratives hold a ' cubic solidity ' beyond his philosophy (XII, 641-2). The assertion is important, since there are sometimes important divergencies between the two. That he should have left his writing to so late an age was consistent with his life-plan, because he did not rate books, even in artistic form, so highly as genius-in-life (VII, 272; IX, 404), and when he agreed that his two literary brothers' style may have been more effective than his own ' *when it was written down* ' (X, 533), the italics sink deep. Christ and Socrates did not write; they spoke; and so did Powys in his prime, speaking like his great predecessors from his whole personality.

However, for us the *Autobiography* remains a book, and we may in conclusion review its findings. The problem of uttermost evil is not solved, nor could it be, here or elsewhere, directly or indirectly. Powys will return to it. With the problem of physical disgusts, on which he lays a heavy emphasis, he appears to have been more successful; and to this too he will return.

There is, as we have seen, the usual Wordsworthian insistence on the livingness of the inanimate, especially when saturated with past human associations, and a belief in thoughts as powers, almost as living entities. He believes in guardian angels or spirit-guides, like Socrates' *daimon* (VIII, 341, 370, 375; IX, 395, 424; X, 472; XI, 602). The existence of a dimension beyond human understanding is uncompromisingly asserted (X, 504; XII, 649-50, 652). The problem of survival is left problematical: Powys is not sure of it (X, 503-4; XII, 619, 642-3, 649-50). As for progress, when socialism has achieved its aim, then, he asks, ' What next? ' The answer is: ' It is then that we want to commune with angels and demons ', ' to worship the elements ', ' to return to the imaginative and poetic life ' which science has killed (X, 494).

World affairs are not directly handled. By so strong a supporter of all the outcasts they hardly could be. Powys's social gospel, like Christ's, though never anti-social, is, so far as externals go, anarchic. His own personality, ranging from clown to sage, is Protean; he is willing to believe in Chance as a main deity; he sees the universe, in the manner of Whitman or William James, as multitudinous, or ' pluralistic '; and he avoids all *tidy* systems. In his support he refers to many time-honoured authorities from Homer to Chinese or Thibetan wisdom. He could enjoy scholastic theology (XII, 630-1), and thrilled, from the age of thirty, to ancient Welsh (VIII, 334-5). His teaching is that of a ' way ', a life-wisdom, or wise-being, such as that defined by Jesus when he said ' *I* am the truth ' (IX, 428). The definition can only exist in terms of personality, and that is precisely why Powys has composed, with so unswerving and unnerving an honesty, this personal account. Nevertheless within the untapped power-sources, the thaumaturgy, here recorded there must lie reservoirs of hope that may eventually transmute mankind, and therefore also the darkest problems, including politics, in which mankind is at present involved.

Perhaps what is most important of all is Powys's way of thinking and living from that exact point where sexual instinct impinges on religious sensibility. Religion, in books of theology, in sermons, or when delivered from what purports to be an authoritative spirit-personality, avoids sexual reference; and perhaps, our embarrassments being what they are, this is necessary. Our most advanced sexual thinking, as in D. H. Lawrence, keeps as close as it can to the physiological and the emotional, avoiding extensions into the occult. The point where the one impinges on the other regularly arouses fear. If we touch it, neither religion nor sexuality will be conventional; the one will draw near to occultism, the other to perversion. We can feel Lawrence, again and again, coming near to this centre, and *sheering off;* and yet here lies the one key to the human enigma. After centuries of mythological, religious, and literary enquiry, Powys, without any dilution of virility and with deep respect maintained to 'the great Phallic Giant' near Cerne Abbas (IV, 132, 138), has, through what he calls his 'masculine-feminine intelligence' (XI, 582), brought the 'psychic-sensuous *Tao*', born of that 'marriage of Psyche and Eros' for which 'so many mystics have groped' (VIII, 341), to full consciousness of some 'Golden Age' (VIII, 364) within the bisexual and 'Saturnian' dimension (VI, 206).

CHAPTER V

Wales, History and Metaphysics

In *A Glastonbury Romance* and *Maiden Castle* darkest evils drew Powys to Welsh mythology, within which the golden secret was felt to be contained. *Morwyn* (1937) attacks the ultimate horror under Welsh guidance.

A typically Powysian hero in North Wales, where Powys himself was now living, is on a walk with Morwyn, her vivisector father, and a dog, when he experiences a strange clairvoyance penetrating Morwyn's mind and a mysterious cataclysm projects them deep within the earth, killing the vivisector but not the others. The event-structure is so devised as to suggest that the hero's Powysian eye-love or eye-lust is in some way related to the dark visionary experiences ahead. Just before the climax Morwyn appears enraptured, becoming like a gipsy-brown, elemental, wild girl. Somehow in her is both the ideal and the horror and the link is nature (see p. 61). The cataclysmic event brings ecstasy to the ' girlish face with elfin ears ' (I, 29).

The Vivisector's ' *eidolon* ' or spirit-body replaces his physical presence and his hideous self is henceforward seen. Other figures appear within a sadists' hell, among them the Marquis de Sade and Torquemada, burner of heretics. Two types of cruelty are emphatic : religious and vivisectional. We watch shoals of sadistic entities crushing to a television apparatus to watch experimental tortures on earth. Our hell is well realised through concrete descriptions of non-physical existence. Talk is silent, almost telepathic, yet not always wholly distinct from language. The setting is half-lit by phosphorescent luminance; snow may be black and air electric; the sky is a solid roof; impressions of adamant, metal and volcanic stone are weighty; colours are brown, dark green, blue-black. There is a subterranean sea. Smells may be sickening. Solidity can be dependent on mind or desire; everything is simultaneously half mental and half material. The realisation of an astral or etheric state is expert.

Our people are saved from the evil hosts by Taliessin who is, we are told, the only person in world-history who visits Hell for intellectual reasons (III, 145). He is searching for the great lost magus Merlin, and recalls that his own poetry touched

> the deepest secret of all in our ancient religion; a secret that bears upon the mystery of good and evil and upon the mystical light that sometimes shines out from the most noisome regions of evil.
>
> (III, 178)

Hell, if ' harrow'd ', or purified, may somehow be made ' a hiding place for the highest ', but only the greatest can so make himself ' a bridge into the future ' (III, 178). The thought is Nietzschean; and certainly literature is usually most powerful when its theme is evil. This truth is immediately illustrated when, plunging to the depths of Hell, they find Merlin beside Cronos, or Saturn, and Cybele the earth-mother, ruler-deities of the old Cretan civilisation, all asleep. We are in the Golden Age, *below* Hell. In ancient Crete, says Taliessin, worship was bloodless, and from there the Grail-worship came to Britain aeons before Christianity. We now have to labour, enriched by the long struggle, to return to this ' Saturnian Age ', learning from Welsh poetry of the ' Paradisaic Underworld ' beyond both ' Hell ' and ' Heaven ' (III, 184).

The atmosphere is aphrodisiac with a ' diffused sensuality ' such as that which Powys's own abnormal sexual approaches are elsewhere said to give; and we are in contact with the etherealised essence of feminine magic (III, 219-20).

So, though the denunciations of cruelty are scathing and the hell-beings hideous, a hope through and beyond, or below, them is glimpsed. When the giant Tityos, whom we may call a variation of the ' Cerne Giant ', and who has been tortured throughout the ages for a nature-prompted (IV, 259) sex-crime, is released, the release, corresponding to the release glimpsed by Holy Sam (p. 37), establishes a sanctification of sexual impulse. Socrates and Rabelais add their voices, the former delivering the gentle gospel of Kwang-Tze*, whom he has met in the Elysian fields. And yet the book's solution, though adumbrated, is not simple. The loved Morwyn elects to accompany her dubiously reformed father's spirit in his earth-bound plans; like Christie in *Wolf Solent,* she is descended from, and preserves filial allegiance to, an evil parent; and our hero, like Adrian

---

* For Kwang-Tze see *A Philosophy of Solitude,* I, 20-2.

Sorio, Wolf Solent, Magnus Muir and Dud No-man, is finally, though not without purpose, alone.

Morwyn is Powys's most dense metaphysical work. We may observe that in attacking his darkest problem he has been forced into an uncompromising assertion of spirit-survival, and that when so forced he handles it as an adept. The final teaching is that Mercy and Pity will win : ' The sleeping-place of the Age of Gold is in the depths of every human heart; and to this must all revert ' (V, 320).

The gold mined in *Morwyn* next suffuses its lustre over the vast narrative *Owen Glendower* (1941), written around Glendower's revolt against Henry IV of England. Powys's mystique of the past colla- borates with his wide historical learning to make of him a half-inspired historical novelist like his own Dud No-man. In earlier novels there was a certain discrepancy between externals and content in that modern realism was felt to bulge and creak from the pressure of eccentric Titans and cosmic powers; but in *Owen Glendower* there is a perfect coalescence of theme and surface. Earlier themes of thauma- turgy, sadism, homosexuality, and bisexual idealism are unobtrusively distributed within a vastly deployed and intricately patterned reading of historical action wherein much that was before felt as extraordinary appears in its new context normal. The territory to be explored is at one point (V, 131) introduced by a mysterious music, rising and falling, like the weird sound in *Maiden Castle* (p. 52).

Owen Glendower is for Wales a national hero; and Powys writes not as a thinker but as one in-love-with his subject, though the ' love ' is the uninvolved, impersonal, and penetrating ' love ' of an artist. We do not suggest, nor does Powys, that the golden age envisaged in *Morwyn* was actually reawakened during the revolt of Glendower; but its presence is nevertheless felt throughout this *tour de force* of Saturnian art. The eye-lust of the *Autobiography* is concentrated as through a lens to burning, sometimes Dantesque, power. The effects have the sharp distinctiveness of medieval art and the colours the defined luminance of stained glass. People's eyes, described again and again in their varied characteristics and colours, are felt as soul- expressions and soul-agents; and costume is variegated and brilliant. Colours are everywhere. Reds and gold predominate. Though nature is grand, and horrors of war, stake and scaffold abound, we are aware primarily of human culture and human civilisation in exact historical perspective.

The human delineation is precise and abundant, including the Thomist scholar Father Pascentius, of darkly penetrating inquisitorial eyes but kindly heart; Master Brut, the young Lollard of almost embarrassing buoyancy, forecast of Protestantism; the one-eyed and subversive prophet Crach Ffinnant; and the woman Lowri of seductive evil. Shakespearian reminiscences are awakened by the sleepless and tormented king, Henry IV; by Hal, whom we meet as a boy; by Sir John Oldcastle, the original of Shakespeare's Falstaff, the points of similarity and difference admirably maintained; and Hotspur. Hotspur is peculiarly interesting, since his personality is the subject of a striking innovation in the art of the historical novel. When Britain is being partitioned in the company of a prophet who in effect functions, albeit unconsciously, as medium, the hero Rhisiart, though Hotspur being dead is not, as he is in Shakespeare, present, sees Hotspur's sword pointing at the map and hears the Shakespearean lines:

> See how this river comes me cranking in,
> And cuts me from the best of all my land
> A huge half-moon, a monstrous cantle out!
>
> (XVII, 663; *1 Henry IV*, III, 1.99)

To Rhisiart what he has experienced is as some mysterious ' ghost out of the future ' beyond his understanding (XVII, 661).

The pervading Christian sensibility touches exquisite apprehensions in Mad Huw, a Franciscan friar for whom Richard II as ' God's wounded rose ' (II, 32) is an ever-present Christ, still living and anxious to save. It is remembered that Richard's fall was, like Edward II's, in part caused by his homosexual tendencies (VII, 199; XIV, 494), and the subtlest flowerings of such delicate attractions receive a medieval pointing in both the girl Tegolin, who accompanies Mad Huw, and the page Elphin. Tegolin is a flame-haired girl for long unobtrusively dominating in strength and love, usually in male dress, and at a high point of ceremonial becoming a Saint Joan, a ' vision ' in ' white and gold ', mounted on a grey charger and in armour, as an ' apotheosis ' beyond all imagination (XVIII, 691 694):

> The warm February sun fell full upon the loosened mass of the girl's flaming hair, hair so thick that it almost hid the gleam of her cuirass, hair so long that it flowed down in blood-red waves upon Seisyll's flanks; while the golden armour covering her breasts and guarding her thighs made all that was visible of her virgin flesh show white as the petals of wood-anemones exposed before their hour amid yellow leaves.
>
> (XVIII, 695)

To balance Tegolin we have the page Elphin, as often in description called 'girlish' as Tegolin is called 'boyish'. He grows from a dangerously (VII, 199) beautiful boy to a sensitive artistic youth as a herald whose bisexual unity idealises its inward adoration into unicorns of heraldic design (XIX, 745-6), to become finally a gentle priest. Here he is, as herald :

> Meanwhile Elphin was assuring them with vehement words that it was impossible that Owen should ever really be defeated. The lad had removed his official costume and stood before them in white tunic and white hosen; and as he lifted up his impassioned face, with the curls falling upon his bare shoulders and the candle-light throwing into relief his rounded hips and slender thighs, it crossed Luned's mind that he looked more like a Herald of Saint Gabriel than of any earthly prince.

(XIX, 748)

White is for Powys a mystical colour (pp. 24, 26, 48). Tegolin and Elphin may be called visionary descendants of Christie and the boys at Lenty Pond in *Wolf Solent*, of Wizzie Ravelton and Larry Zed. Human warmth is replaced by radiance and idealisation, but the radiance is electric. Both, and the 'womanish' (XVIII, 685) Mad Huw, are bisexually imagined, the Platonic intuitions of the *Autobiography* attaining a new meaning, as *Wolf Solent* at one point forecast (XVI, 357 or 340), in a *medieval* context. Powys is using psychological experiences which outspace our century's conventions to recreate a period wherein they held a greater authority.

The process is even clearer in treatment of Owen himself. Much of his reputation as a magician is accepted as superstitious, but there is a genuine core to it in his use of soul-projection, for which Powys draws on his own experience; and though this is developed on one occasion to the power of rendering himself visible to others at a distance (XXI, 904-6, 913-14), there are precedents for such manifestations, including a story told of Powys himself (p. 128). There is much else in Owen as man of culture and as statesman, the varied strains composing a figure of historical conviction. For once, and the exception is typical of *Owen Glendower*, a Powys miracle-man or sage is handsome; whereas all the others are excessively ugly. Owen has a golden-tinted beard, and wears golden accoutrements and golden robes. He is once compared to a 'golden image' (XIV, 511).

Despite these impressions there is no sentimentalisation. Tegolin, like Christie and Morwyn, comes from a dark parentage, the evil Lowri.

Owen is as a leader indecisive and he commits an act of sadistic cruelty (XIII, 438-40). Elphin lacks courage. The Powys-hero Rhisiart, though as sexually indecisive as his predecessors — he enjoys an experience of ' diffused ' love with Tegolin (VII, 250) — is more objectively created as a well-meaning but dullish young intellectual with instincts for power whose final attaining to the position of a high court judge under Henry V is as strikingly unexpected as it is entirely convincing.

Nature, though not allowed to suffuse the story, is exactly placed in a number of exquisite descriptions attuned to the narrative. Here is a description of dawn before the battle of Bryn Glas, a marvel of exact perceptual reportage which simultaneously presents a movement from red to gold in accord with the book's dominant colourings :

> Irregular blood-red streaks appeared now in the eastern quarter. One second and there were none of these; another second and there they were ! And with the coming of these blood-red streaks the air that cooled their faces suddenly lost a certain damp chill that characterized it before; and though it didn't grow warm it carried with it a perceptible quality of *livingness,* as if those red streaks in the sky, wild and sad as they were, like a reflection from battle-fields of long ago, brought with them something familiar, some-thing steeped in old earth-memories, that drove back the mortal death-chill of the empty night.
>
> By degrees, as they watched, they perceived that these dark-red streaks had changed their character. They didn't see them in the process of changing, for it is forbidden to the human eye to catch the actual movement of celestial presences, but where they'd been contemplating dark blood-streaks they were now contemplating rose-coloured clouds ! Nor was it long as they watched — and even the five horses seemed to be expanding their nostrils towards the east — before that rose-tinge had spread over the whole sky till it reached the zenith, while in the quarter where the blood-streaks had first appeared it was as if some vast magic gates had opened, leading into an infinity of glorified distance, into a receding perspective of golden space.

(XV, 547)

After the battle there is a ' shapeless moon ', by whose ' phantom light ' Rhisiart witnesses the hideous desecration of English corpses by a band of women ' working obscene and monstrous blasphemy upon the very secrets of creation ' (XV, 555-6).

Growing from nature, and more especially from its inanimate forms, from the stones and slate and mists of North Wales, is the gaunt and giant figure of Broch-o'-Meifod, who represents the ancient Welsh stock in comparison with which Owen himself is regarded as a half-breed; who believes in death, by which he means death-as-death, and in the powers of the elements; and who claims that a new revelation beyond the Christian is yet to come. In him are strands from the Jobber and Uryen Quirm and he incarnates much of Powys's subsequent philosophy; but he remains a peripheral figure; he is not allowed to blur the medieval and bisexual idealisms; and the Sun dominates. The book has an exact, tragic, form, rising to imaginative splendours at Harlech, and then falling. Once Broch, limbs glistening from the waters of Harlech, becomes an aureoled and sun-sparkling figure (XIX, 774; and see XVII, 633), touching that blend of sea and sun which Sylvanus Cobbold regarded as the ultimate revelation and which for Powys himself opened Nirvana (*Autobiography*, IV, 145).

Owen Glendower might be called Powys's greatest *artistic* achievement; a maximum of its contents in human insight, historical learning and intuition, archaeological exactitude, theological disquisition, social understanding both of the past and as pointing to modern advances, all can be fully received without reference to Powys's other works, though the relation is there. In it he allows full scope to idealisms, Christian and bisexual, that do not again recur. The quality of his artistic achievement in *Owen Glendower* is happily defined during a description of a Bard's heroic rhapsody in celebration of Owen's revolt:

> As the man's voice rose in his wild excitement the notes of the harp seemed sometimes to follow, sometimes to lead his utterance; but what Rhisiart, as he listened, found most extraordinary was the way a certain hard, clear, conscious, almost cold *intention* continued to retain in the midst of the wildest excursions of his frenzy the symphonic unity of his performance.
> He went back upon himself, he gathered up his earlier motifs, he reverted to those hummings and whisperings, like the vague stirrings in the air of thousands of summer afternoons. He reverted to the screaming of eagles, to the pipings of curlews, to the cawings of rooks.
> Into the rhythm of the hooves of Owen's war-horse, into the rush of the flying track of that flamingo feather, into the cleaving of skulls under that broken sword, he tossed the roar of the falling cataracts he had plundered, he flung the wailing of the journeying winds he had invoked.
> Rhisiart couldn't follow all the words he used. Many of them were old archaic words, words borrowed from Taliessin, from Aneurin, from Llywarch Hen. Some of them he suspected to be

words coined for the occasion by the Bard himself. Nor could he follow all the strange rhythms of the accompaniment. Many of these seemed to him to be conjured up out of the very abysses of prehistoric time. He heard the crashing of ice-floes in the glacial era; he heard the moaning of winds in forests roamed by mammoths; he heard the hissing of the lava in prehistoric volcanoes as it was drowned in the tidal waves of nameless seas.

(VI, 156)

This is not quite the imaginative territory of *Owen Glendower* as a whole; it is nearer that of *Porius*. It does however define what Shakespeare called the 'dark backward and abysm', the temporal hinterland, of our story, wherein we have reminders — not in terms of a 'golden' age to avoid rivalry with the medieval splendours — of a bloodless age recalling *Maiden Castle,* to which Owen himself is distantly related (XII, 419; XIX, 760; XXI, 889, 911); and when the bardic power becomes so great that *the Bard himself becomes invisible,* we have a neat correspondence to Powys's own present artistry. For it seems that by power of love, love of Wales, and also of the medieval period, his titanic self has been subdued to an impersonal, Shakespearian, art independent of and yet including his self-dedicated quest; and that in consequence the longed-for Saturnian secret has been, in artistic terms, revealed.*

Mortal Strife (1941), perhaps Powys's most satisfying metaphysical survey, was written during the war to encourage the people of Britain. Love, being possessive, is rejected in favour of the less spectacular virtues of kindliness, cheerfulness and humility, together with the British type of humour. These are contrasted to their advantage with the tense and towering ambitions of Hitler's Germany; for it is such seemingly 'poor-spirited' qualities that 'go to make an unconquerable person' (IX, 145).

British humour taps 'a spiritual force that comes from outside the astronomical universe' (IX, 158), and *Mortal Strife* throughout regards man as an 'amphibious' (X, 169) creature already half within a dimension beyond normal perception. It can be touched, despite all but the worst sufferings, by the technique of semi-erotic (IX, 148) self-blending, or diffusion, into external objects, whatever they be, though perhaps especially rich when impregnated with racial memories

---

* My more detailed examination of *Owen Glendower* appears in *A Review of English Literature,* IV. 1 (January, 1963).

(IX, 142). *Mortal Strife* surveys mysteries beyond time, beyond life
and death :

> What in this Dimension we naturally think and feel about life
> and death is in harmony with this Dimension. When we are dead,
> life and death, according to this present dimension, cease; and
> something else substitutes itself for them. Of the nature of this
> something else it is not only now impossible to obtain the faintest
> clue; it must of necessity always be impossible, simply because
> Time and Space *get in the way.*
>
> (VII, 113)

We are not bound merely for a ' life after death ', but for ' something
much more like a million lives after death ', the thing beyond being
the exact opposite of ' Nothingness ' (VIII, 134, 136). Powys's
optimism is here in line with Whitman's, so admirably discussed in
The Pleasures of Literature (1938; the relevant passages are omitted in
the American edition).

The Kwang-Tze virtues of humility and humour are blended with
Powys's recurring stress on the more simple enjoyments of mortal
existence : ' My claim is that the natural way, the intended way, the
Utopian and Golden Age way, of enjoying life is by a cult of sensations ' (X, 168); by which Powys does not mean ' the sensational '.
That his gospel of courage, kindliness and humour was actually being
lived by him at this period is witnessed by his letters to Louis
Wilkinson (pub. 1958). The war seems to have empowered his
visionary thought.

In *The Art of Growing Old* (1944) he is equally emphatic on the
existence of other dimensions beyond sense-perception, asserting that
it is positively ' laughable to regard this present space-time barrier as
the end and final high-tide-mark of all possible existence ' (VIII, 128).
This is not ' mysticism ', but the simplest common-sense (VII, 109).
Human survival is supported. Everywhere we see the positives winning
over the negatives and since the ' life-sap ' of the essential personality
seems to be stronger than the physical ' death-slide ', survival is likely
(XII, 212-13). Man is set between the vast inanimate and external
and the inward abysms of his own mind; the first we must *enjoy,*
the second is the power-source of goodness (VI, 103-5). From these
two ultimates Powys derives his two commandments : ' *Enjoy all :
be kind to all* ' (VI, 98; VII, 117).

Mortal Strife and *The Art of Growing Old* differ from Powys's
other metaphysical books — among which I do not include the more

generalised survey of *The Meaning of Culture* — in their range of human interest and urbanity of approach. Discussions on men and women, on sexual instinct, on politics, world-movements, and religion radiate from Powys's central wisdom, the general tenor being a respect for the humble and the ordinary, and a repudiation, *in whatever guise they come,* of forced systems and dictatorial pride. There is, as in *Owen Glendower,* a new realism and objectivity; and there is a new optimism regarding the ultimate destinies of man. It is as though the shadowing presence and attendant power of war-time Death had attuned Powys uniquely to the mysteries beyond, from whence he drew assurance to present his two-fold counsel of enjoyment and kindliness within a context of metaphysical serenity.

Probably Powys was also drawing strength from his residence in North Wales. As we have seen, he usually relates his ' Golden Age ' to ancient Welsh wisdom, as in *Maiden Castle* and *Morwyn.* Reasons for his Welsh allegiance are given throughout *Obstinate Cymric* (1947; essays written from 1935 to 1947).

Powys discusses theories that trace the aboriginal Welsh to non-Aryan and pre-Celtic Berbers from North Africa : Taliessin claimed to derive his magical cosmology not from Asia but from Africa (IV, 49-51; VI, 75-6; X, 171). Another possible source may have been Cretan, the Welsh fertility goddess Ceridwen representing the Earth-Mother of ancient Crete, whose worship was bloodless (V, 59-60; VI, 73, 83). Africa and Crete appear to share jointly the honours of a life-way ' contemporary with lost Atlantis ' (I, 9), and the result in Wales has been a typically Powysian cluster of virtues and values : a reserved mysticism impervious to conquests which survives in the music, gesture and intonation of Welsh speech — we remember Powys's own dithyrambic lecturing — whatever foreign *words* they may have been forced to assimilate; a tendency towards the communal and towards the matriarchal; a poetic and reverential belief in the Eternal Feminine as a cosmic power hostile to man-made systems, and in elementals such as sylphs, gnomes, undines and salamanders; and by a preference of little things to great causes. Powys detects certain resemblances between the Welsh and China. Their mountain-strongholds and sage-like manner recall Thibet (IV, 52; V, 62). Deep within is some ' Saturnian ' (VI, 73) and elusive ' secret of life ' (VI, 82), for the customs and ways of this ancient Welsh race still retain ' memories of the Golden Age when Saturn, or some megalithic philosopher under that name, ruled in Crete, and the Great Mother was worshipped without the shedding of blood ' (VI, 83).

In the essay (VII) ' Pair Dadeni ' or ' the Cauldron of Rebirth ', published in 1946 and included in *Obstinate Cymric*, Powys notes the Welsh tendency to mix up life and death ' so that on all sides we grow aware of half-alive things and of half-dead things, of life vanishing as the death mists rise or fall, of birth appearing even from the lap of death ' (VII, 86). Of this comprehensive if misty wisdom Uryen Quirm was a prophet and it relates to Broch's elemental stone-wisdom in *Owen Glendower*. In ' Pair Dadeni ' it is associated with the esoteric doctrine of the passing of two thousand troubled years under the sign Pisces to make way for a more feminine and less tensely intellectual culture under Aquarius : this will be the ' Aquarian Age '. Powys's association of the Red Army with earth-worship, Demeter and the Mother of God in the Greek Church accompanies a rejection of State-Communism as no less cynical and pitilessly despotic than the Big Business it claims to improve upon (VII, 110; X, 154). What he is searching for finds no equivalent in any contemporary *system*. In the Renaissance, called a movement from above rather than below, ' the great Mother miscarried ' (VII, 102).

His pluralistic and anarchistic philosophy is more and more tending towards the un-ideal and the un-systematic. He is — we are now at writing subsequent to *The Art of Growing Old* — less ready to be involved in imponderables. Love and the Church are rejected in favour of the ' magnanimous and indulgent common-sense ' of Homer, Aristophanes, Rabelais and Goethe (X, 140). Nevertheless he himself continues his life-long habit of prayer, to Taliessin and others, and directs healing thought-waves to man and animal. The question of human survival now interests him less, but drawing on his habitual experience of soul-exteriorization he thinks it possible, though thought must have some body, if only an electronic one, and the apparent independence of the physical exists in a different degree from other independencies (X, 154-9). The soul has two sides, like Uryen's moon, light and dark, drawing strength from the dark, though locked in space and time. ' Eternity ' is unimaginable; space and time forbid it; and though he had said as much in *Mortal Strife* Powys's thoughts regarding a beyond appear to be growing more agnostic, if not slightly hostile (X, 159-62). Goodness is possible without reliance on a moral authority beyond this dimension, and the dark hinterland of the soul is even

called a void (X, 166-7, 177-8). Repudiating materialism as normally understood and also determinism, he reasserts his belief in a
' way ' near to Taoism and the *essence* of Christianity, but only in so
far as they are taken experimentally and not as systems; or perhaps,
remembering Taliessin, the secret may — Powys is probably also recalling his loved American negroes — be African or Iberian (X, 171-3).
He sums himself up as ' a periphrastic Pantagruelist converted by
Wales and Welsh mythology into an Aristophanic Feminist ' (X, 167).

In *Obstinate Cymric* we are reminded that Owen Glendower was a
Normandised Celt for whom the Aboriginals shed their blood, and
that the true stock must always return to the earth for reinvigoration
(I, 12; IV, 53). Of this more primitive and elemental strength
Broch-o'-Meifod was the impersonation, though he remained no more
than a peripheral figure. In *Porius* (1951) Powys searches back to a
period more deeply attuned to his developing Cymric philosophy.

We are in the early sixth century, a thousand years before
Glendower, when the same terrain of North Wales was the scene of
multi-racial rivalries and interpenetrations. In the forefront are the
Celtic Brythons, supposed descendants of the Trojans, in part Roman-
ised; around are the ' anarchical and peaceful ' race of the ' Forest
People ', descended from the Iberians of North Africa; the yet earlier
and mysterious Ffichtiaid (Picts) who had afterwards allied themselves with the savage Gwyddylaid (Scots); and even members of the
ancient giant race, the Cewri (xi; I, 1-3, 14-15; X, 152-3; XVI,
307-8; XVIII, 380, 389-90; XX, 433; XXII, 505, 519). The Emperor
Arthur and his knights stand for Romano-British rule in opposition
to yet another race, the invading Saeson or Saxons. There are linger-
ing, but still active, representatives, in the three sovereign Aunts of
the Brython prince Einion, of an age-old matriarchal authority
(XVI, 307-8).

People are close to earth, living in stone fortresses, wooden huts,
skin-tents, and caves, some actually in subterranean retreats. There
are reminders of hunting, and wild animals such as the wolf, badger,
fox and stags are vivid. There is a prevailing sense, typical of Powys
but here more than usually organic, of reptilian or other cold-blooded
life such as serpents, toads, and frogs. We are in thick forest and other
vegetation, tangled with brushwood and undergrowth and our feet
sinking into leaf-mould. Those old Powysian favourites, bracken,
fungus, moss and lichen, are more than ever dominant : it is as though

the half-fungoid personality of Uryen Quirm were being expanded
to suffuse a world. Earth is sodden as we move through bogs and
marshes. Much of the action is around Lake Tegid, or Bala, and its
reedy banks; and the river Dee interthreads as a sacred entity. Beyond,
to the west, are the great mountains. Action is swathed in mists, and
in particular by a corpse-odoured straw-coloured mist coming from
Cader Idris. Instead of the reds and golds of *Owen Glendower* our
main colours are green and yellow, especially yellow. But colours,
though often mentioned, are not assertive, nor is light. The sun is for
long less effective than the moon, or perhaps even the stars, though
it shares ambiguous honour with the sickly straw-coloured mist towards
the end.

Among these forests and marshes and mists seethes nevertheless an
intense intellectual activity. The racial mingling throws up the froth
of religious and philosophic controversy. The range is wide, covering
orthodox Christianity, Pelagian heresy, Mithraism, Pythagoreanism,
and Judaism. We have a solitary Druid. Classical culture and literature
— Aristophanes, Plato, Virgil, Ovid — are near-distance powers.
Myths and cultures jostle and push. We watch people struggling to
disentangle themselves from earth-life to civilisation and from super-
stition to religion, though we are never sure how far this disentangling
may be an advance and whether truth lies in the future or in the
past. On this northern corner of Europe fall influences from the
Mediterranean, from Rome, ancient Greece, and earlier, sometimes
from a lost golden age.

Such a book is not easy reading. The detailed historical knowledge
is so dense that it clogs the action, and we are often more aware of
historical atmosphere than of historical events. Part of the trouble
comes from our expecting historical excitements where the author has
no intention of providing them. Though Arthur is a brilliant cameo
in military genius absorbed in war, the equal of Julius Caesar or Han-
nibal (XVII, 352), he remains a miniature, and Powys's refusal of
conventional idealism, which may be allowed to include the medieval
excellences of *Owen Glendower,* makes of Arthur's followers a set of
effeminate young men out-of-place in their grim setting; while the
boy Galahad, no more of a warrior than Elphin, is pitiful in battle
(XXI, 475-8). This battle, for which we had waited as a climax,
is statically presented; we are told that arrows fly, but we are more
vividly aware, with a kind of Tolstoyan deflation, of a riderless and

terrified horse madly interthreading the conflict accompanied by a howling dog (XXI, 476).

Again, since Powys's explicit philosophy now refuses so many distinctions of great and small, seeing miracles in minutiae, we must expect, from so god-like a view — the view of Browning's Lazarus in his *Epistle of Karshish* — many a shift in emphasis. Our exponent here, following Sylvanus Cobbold's equation of the Absolute with ' Everything ' (p. 46), is the young poet-prodigy Taliessin himself, one of Arthur's followers. He proclaims a gospel which is the inevitable death of dramatic emphasis :

> The ending forever of the Guilt-sense and God-sense,
> The ending forever of the Sin-sense and Shame-sense,
> The ending forever of the Love-sense and Loss-sense,
> The beginning forever of the Peace paradisic,
> The ' I feel ' without question, the ' I am ' without purpose,
> The ' It is ' that leads nowhere, the life with no climax,
> The ' Enough ' that leads forward to no consummation,
> The answer to all things, that yet answers nothing,
> The centre of all things, yet all on the surface,
> The secret of Nature, yet Nature goes blabbing it
> With all of her voices from earth, fire, air, water !
> Whence comes it? Whither goes it? It is nameless; it is shameless;
> It is Time free at last from its Ghostly Accuser,
> Time haunted no more by a Phantom Eternal;
> It is Godless; but its gods are as sea-sands in number;
> It's the Square with four sides that encloses all circles;
> Four horizons hath this Tetrad that swallows all Triads;
> It includes every creature that Nature can summon.
> It excludes from Annwfyn nor man, beast, nor woman !
>
> (XIX, 417)

This is Powys's clearest statement of his later philosophy in distinction from a systematic and monistic theology. After his rhapsody Taliessin relaxes into ' an intimate relation ' with the first ' small inanimate object ' that catches his eye.

Merlin, here called ' Myrddin Wyllt ', is presented as a magician of extraordinary powers, of which perhaps the chief is his telepathic communication with animals and the attraction he exerts on them, so that the forest creatures come from their lairs to cluster around him. He is, like his Powys predecessors, massive in bulk and appallingly ugly, with enormous ears, black African hair and green cavernous eyes. He exudes, like Uryen Quirm, a fungoid death-odour. He appears to people in different shapes; sometimes he seems more like an old woman than a man (III, 57-8). His 'organism' possesses a 'conscious recession into its primordial beginnings' and constitutes 'a multiple identity composed of many separate lives', including beasts, birds, reptiles, vegetation and stone (III, 58-9). He has prophetic powers (VI, 99-100), and is a 'medium' for unseen forces (VI, 105). He is almost as much animal as man, and sometimes seems sub-human. But he also constitutes a challenge, such as that defined by Taliessin's lines, on all tyrannic systems. The events of the chapter 'Myrddin Wyllt' occur aptly on Saturday, or 'Saturn's Day' (XV, 265), for his mind journeys over huge spaces of time and he thinks that he is a reincarnation of Cronos, or Saturn, the ruler who overthrew a tyrant god to give men and beasts the Golden Age (XV, 275-285). He can however be uncertain of himself and asks Mother Earth to tell him who he is. He is not happy; he bears the sufferings of animals and of men through aeons of time, and can long for death (XV, 281-7; XIX, 412). His thoughts and movements are heavy and cumbrous as the movement of the book in which he lives.

When in danger from enemies he falls down, head foremost, 'thrusting his soul' into the earth (XV, 298), like Uryen Quirm. This is his position during the battle while his opposition to orthodoxy is being defined, in one of Powys's finest pieces of denunciatory rhetoric, by a fanatical Christian priest:

> Oh, how that unholy, huddled-up monstrous toad hates the very name of the Blessed Trinity! He has even dared to declare, as Christ's poor servants in Caerwynt and Caerlleon and Caerloyw and Caerlyr have told me, that one of the worst of these devils in human flesh that those thrice-accurst Greeks called 'Philosophers', a prize-devil, a master-devil, a dragon-tailed devil, a great ramping, roaring, ram's-horn devil called Pythagoras, swore that the number *four* and not the number *three* was the secret of God's most holy cosmos! Yes! Yes! Yes! That cowering lump of Satan's dung over there, calling in vain upon Hell to aid him — he is the cause — he alone and only he is the cause, of the landing of the Saeson on these shores! Ride over him, horsemen of the Emperor! Loose your arrows upon him, People of the Forest!
>
> (XXI, 482)

Either through his opposers' earth-magic or the force of his own paroxysm, the priest falls dead. The philosophic implications of Myrddin Wyllt's wisdom, which corresponds to Taliessin's, recall Whitman's 'Square Deific'. The contrast of Three and Four is the contrast of unitary system against plurality.

The action of *Porius* is hampered; the events, together with past aeons of suggested time, are crushed within a single week, and a world of races within a single novel. The concentration falls so heavily on a massively spatial ' now ' that narrative is constricted; everything is at every instant being seen and felt statically and in depth. *Space contains time;* and of this crushing together and containment the Protean Myrddin Wyllt is a personification.

And yet once, and once only, the narrative is freed. Porius is here the Powys-hero. He is sexually impeded (IV, 74; XXII, 491-3; XXIII, 530), and like Wolf in *Wolf Solent* enjoys a secret sensuous-mystical habit which he calls ' cavoseniargizing ' (V, 81, 93; VI, 106; IX, 146; X, 169, XIX, 396, 402-3.* He is introverted and indecisive (VIII, 120-1). But his descent is traced both to Iberian stock and to the Cewri, the Giants; and he is of giant, though clumsy, strength. Powys-heroes have not hitherto been, like the magicians, massive, and since in Powys the physical tends to symbolise the soul-quality, the conception of the semi-giant Porius may suggest that former Powys-heroes have been ineffectual only through a dormant strength, symbolised by Dud No-man's ' Cerne Giant stick ' (p. 50) and now in Porius finding its true level. Their sex-impulses were too expansive, too diffused, as Dud No-man explained (p. 50 above), for normal intercourse. Now in *Porius* two last representatives of the aboriginal giant race appear from Cader Idris, a man and his yellow-haired daughter. The hitherto indecisive Porius, seeing the daughter, becomes at last a man of decision and ' *action* '. Simultaneously he recognises ' the primal mystery of the different consciousness of male and female ' (XXII, 512-3, 518; and see XX, 458). In other words, finding a giant mate, *the Powys-hero becomes both normal and heroic.* Mind and body are now distinct, mind ruling (XXII, 512); sexual and other differentiations succeed fusion. The bisexuality of *Owen Glendower,* medieval and Christian, is in *Porius* slighted; feared in the femininely beautiful Drom (XIV, 244, 246, 264) as a ' Jesus-lad ' (XXVI, 611) of inhuman spirituality (XXV, 598-9); repellent in the effete Llew (XIV, 241; XXIII, 530); just admitted in Arthur himself (XVII, 356, 358), but questioned in his followers (I, 22-7; XIX, 394). Merlin's page Neb-ap-Digon is given no such erotic tinge as had Elphin in *Owen*

---

* The word, which suggests cave ', ' energising ' and perhaps ' enlarge ', appears to derive from an incident insufficiently described, perhaps through the heavy cutting of the text for publication. The giants come from mountain caves (XX, 433; XXII, 519).

Glendower, and Taliessin is specifically not bi-sexual but 'a-sexual' (XIX, 414). That the new mode chimes exactly with Taliessin's non-unitary gospel is clear from the violently anti-Christian aspersions on Drom as a monistic symbol (XXV, 599).

So now we have our climax, more epic than dramatic, for which the story has been labouring. The scene is set by the elements. The sun has been golden, but also 'a chill of a peculiar kind' has been accompanied by the arrival from the direction of Cader Idris, whence the Cewri come, of a 'wet, cold, clammy, straw-coloured mist', such as we have met before and which may be supposed to have been forecasting this climax (XXI, 485). It is within this blending of sun-and-mist that Porius approaches the 'goddess' giant of his 'secretest broodings' (XXII, 517; and see I, 20; XI, 199; XIX, 411), and enjoys union with her, drawing strength as from the elements themselves. For they are *akin*:

> An unfulfilled craving was in each of them — the deep sex-yearning of one primeval form of matter for another primeval form of matter.
> (XXII, 519)

The father approaches; there is a fight. The girl interposes, the giant's knotted club crashes on her head, and he utters at Porius

> a wild and terrible word, the reverberation of which no living man at whom it was aimed could ever forget; and Porius never did forget its psychic vibration, though of the syllables that composed it he remembered nothing, for it was a long scaly word like the hissing of a dragon heard through miles of marshy reeds; and Porius could feel its deadly venom, like the spittle of an insane incubus, strike ice-cold against his cheek.
> (XXII, 521)

After the girl has been thus accidentally killed, Porius pursues the giant, who carries his daughter's body up the mountain-side and plunges to his death in a tarn, shattering himself and the girl's corpse. There is a wild and cold beauty in the 'sun-illumined depths of emerald-green water' (XXII, 523) where they sink. Porius is staggered by the vision:

> And the river of time carried him away up the centuries, up thousands upon thousands of centuries, till he was permitted to behold in his own person the terrestrial catastrophe which caused this almost bottomless mountain-lake to be formed, and this prison of submerged rock to make captive these two corpses.
> (XXII, 524)

Henceforth 'those two pairs of open eyes staring up at him through blood and hair and green water' is to constitute for Porius his dream-voyage ' into another world ' (XXIII, 538).

So, through yellowish mist, green depths, and sunlight, Powys realises the terror, violence and fascination, the pathos and mystery, of this giant race towards which his thought has so often, as in his persistent interest in the Cerne Giant, been directed.

And at the end, when Porius has laboured to rescue Myrddin Wyllt from his burial on y Wyddfa, or Snowdon, called ' the peaktomb of Cronos ' (XXII, 521), and the magician has given him a restorative draught, Porius' sense of the ' second Age of Gold ' which is being planned by Myrrdin for the liberation of suffering creation and ' the Saturnian nepenthe ' he has himself drunk are associated with the remembered sight of the dead giants (XXIX, 681).

In *The Inmates* (1952) Wales as a source of occult wisdom is replaced by Thibet. Thibetan occultism, to which a good introduction is W. Y. Evans-Wentz's famous *The Tibetan Book of the Dead*, has been often in Powys's thought, in the *Autobiography* and elsewhere (e.g. pp. 45, 63, 74 above). Our new sage is Morsimmon Esty, called ' the man from Thibet '.

The setting is Dr Echetus's mental home which, like the asylum in *Jobber Skald,* has a vivisectional laboratory attached. The home with its two clerics, Fathers Wun and Toby, Catholic and Protestant, symbolises life as a madhouse and torture-chamber under a monistic theology. Morsimmon Esty, who has arrived from Thibet, is in ' full evening dress ' and has, as successor to Uryen Quirm and Myrddin Wyllt, a gargoyle skull-face, gorilla-like proportions and a ' hardly human ' voice suggestive of an insect (XIII, 241). Like Myrddin Wyllt he is less a person than a multitude of life-forms, and he asserts a doctrine of pluralism, believing in the likelihood of millions of universes unknown and inapproachable by us, but none of it ' eternal ' (XIII, 241-3).

John Hush, the hero, is, as was Adrian Sorio in *Rodmoor,* a mental patient, and loves another patient, the girl Tenna, seeing her in Powysian fashion as a sylph or undine. His abnormality goes so far as a terrified obsession that he is himself turning into a woman (XIV, 247-9). While attempting an escape, John is in danger from Dr Echetus's sadistic vivisectional assistant Gewlie, who is a fanatical believer in One God. Under, it seems, the influence of the Thibet-man John experiences a clairvoyant insight, recalling the psychical X-ray effects of *Morwyn*, into the ' millions of little clock-cells in Gewlie's skull that were ticking and tinkling and turning their tiny wheels on their electric pivots '; he actually *saw* them. He reads Gewlie's thoughts, but this is done by unmediated mental reception, and *not from the clockwork* (XIV, 258-9). He also saw ' the insubstantial and yet not quite immaterial soul-covering or soul-skin ', half-way between ' visible ' and ' invisible ', which looks like

> a cloudy shape in the form of a man, composed of semi-transparent mist, the colour of a puddle of dirty water upon which has just fallen some dark purplish shadow.
>
> (XIV, 258)

He could also see the link, at the nape of the neck, between soul and body, chemically composed and like a ' living eel '. It was shown as

> something distinct from both Gewlie's spirit and Gewlie's flesh by the peculiar way it quivered and shivered, and still more by the extraordinary manner in which like a thin little inlet of sea-water in wind-swept sand it kept being traversed from end to end by rippling vibrations just as if it were swallowing something not much smaller than itself!
>
> (XIV, 259)

This is the ' silver cord ' of Thibetan, and indeed Biblical (*Ecclesiastes*, XII, 6), teaching, well-known to occultism. John is made aware of what ' thunderbolts of power lay in the miserablest human soul ' and felt like worshipping the divine in all, even the lowest, humanity (XIV, 261).

Morsimmon Esty has the powers, resembling those possessed by Prospero — to whom he once refers (XIII, 243) — and those aimed at by Shaw's Captain Shotover in *Heartbreak House*, of directing mind rays to paralyse an opponent. He can do more. Appearing on the scene as not merely an ' overwhelming personality ' but almost as ' a supernatural apparition ', he begins, functioning as a personification of Death, to *disintegrate* Gewlie, who in the process experiences an ' ecstatic happiness ' (XV, 273). The Thibet man's association with Death is driven home by his having his back turned to John, who cannot see his face (XV, 273, 276), so corresponding to our many passages where the death-mystery is regarded as a hidden *other side,* sometimes of the moon (see pp. 54, 112).

What exactly happens to Gewlie's soul is left ambiguous :

> The flame of that soul had curled itself up like a crouching tiger within the cauldron of the wretch's cruelty; but now it was released.

It had leapt up. It had leapt out. The infernal cat was out of the holy bag.

(XV, 274)

There may be the implication that the released soul will be more dangerous than the soul imprisoned in flesh. John's thoughts, following Geard of Glastonbury (*A Glastonbury Romance* XXX, 1136-8 or 1084-6) and some aspects of Thibetan lore, wonder if at death we pass from dream to dream, never touching solid ground (XV, 275). Morsimmon Esty's apparent assertion of death as complete annihilation earlier (XIII, 243) cannot be readily assimilated with these later suggestions, though he certainly has the power, recalling *Ducdame*, of so directing some ' devolutionary cosmic ray ' as to magnetise people down through animal and vegetable to gases and atoms (XV, 279). John once himself recovers from the Thibetan's mesmeric paralysing by contact with the earth, moving, like an animal, on all fours, as did Uryen Quirm. The man's — if they are a man's — powers are exerted less drastically against Father Wun and Father Toby, the Catholic having a reserve of faith to support him in excess of the Protestant's.

These strange events are accompanied by typical descriptions of mist and dawn, as the sun rises above the earth-works of an ancient camp. *The Inmates* is Powys's furthest adventure, following *Morwyn*, of concrete, spiritualistic, apprehension, which in both appears to be intimately related to, if not actually conditioned by, the vivisectional horror.

CHAPTER VI

A New Gospel

Parallel to Powys's darker intuitions, which gave us his penetrating study *Dostoievsky* (1946), runs his Whitmanesque gospel of pluralistic optimism, reaching its culmination in his *Rabelais* (1948). Extracts are translated and a long commentary appended on the kathartic acceptances of Rabelais' humour.

For long Powys has concentrated on both lower life-forms in nature and the physically repellent in man. His magicians and prophets are gross, and, like the Grail messenger in legend, ugly. Disgust may be an obsession, as in *Rodmoor* (XV, 201-5), and is strong in the *Autobiography*. Wolf in *Wolf Solent* and Sam in *A Glastonbury Romance* win insight through excremental acceptance and anal mysticism, the latter attaining thereby a glimpse of universal liberation for the world's 'tormented flesh' (p. 37 above). Geard's Grail-insight is accompanied by his 'Bugger me black' and Sylvanus Cobbold's mastery of physical repellence is signalled by his manner of introducing himself to his 'Absolute' as 'Caput-Anus'. When Mr Evans finds in the old poem 'The Harrying of Annwn' a mysterious release (stated also by Taliessin in *Morwyn*, p. 66 above) for one who 'understands it', what he was privately envisaging was like some 'monstrous Rabelaisian jest' (XXV, 843 or 807-8). Our key-statement comes in the 1955 preface to *A Glastonbury Romance*, where, writing of the Grail, Powys tells us:

> Only those who have caught the secret which Rabelais more than anyone else reveals to us, the secret of the conjunction of the particular and extreme grossness of our excremental functions in connection with our sexual functions are on the right track to encompass this receding horizon where the beyond-thought loses itself in the beyond-words.
>
> (xv)

The union is a kind of union of life-and-death, and Powys's Magus-figures are sometimes corpse-like in appearance and even odour. Mastery of the repellent is a step, if not to understanding of death, at

85

least to a mastery of its horror. This is a God-like, artistic acceptance, as when in *A Glastonbury Romance* Powys describes without preference ' thought-elementals ' clustering round an embryo as blow-flies attracted to carrion or humming-bird moths to carnations (XXIX, 1080 or 1032). We remember that Sylvanus Cobbold's Absolute was equated with ' All there was ' (p. 46 above). The classic example of this acceptance is the release of Coleridge's Ancient Mariner after he has learned to bless the reptilian sea-creatures.

Stalwart figures such as Lord Carfax in *Wolf Solent,* the Jobber and Broch-o'-Meifod, are created from a not dissimilar viewpoint, and Broch's statement that only when we accept the physically repellent, as did the ancient people of Wales, can ' this " spirit " they talk about ' — the next words are ambiguous — ' float clear away ' (*Owen Glendower* XXI, 920-1) is a key to Powys's doctrine.

Powys sees Rabelais as the great and generous prophet of a new consciousness expanding the acceptances of comedy to a universal wisdom. The comic, as Nietzsche too insisted, must henceforth be included in our religious apprehensions. Geard agreed to having a clown in the Glastonbury Passion-Play; Sylvanus Cobbold's brother was a famous clown; and Powys sees himself as a ' zany ' (*Autobiography,* X, 537-8). Clowning is a medium through which we may accept what would be otherwise intolerable.

After two thousand years of love-idealism and their concomitant hates, systems, tortures and the worship of agony under the sign Pisces, Powys's Rabelais introduces the age of Aquarius, to be characterised by common-sense and kindliness and a child-like and shameless acceptance, worshipping instead of a tyrannic deity life in all its multifarious manifestations. In the process taboos of sex, religion and the family are correspondingly slighted and mocked. The new wisdom is to come from below rather than from above and it is to this extent, like Whitman's, democratic if not proletarian, so that, though systems are rejected, he may be called ' the humorous prophet of the new Federation of the World ' (VII, 359). Anarchy is the political equivalent, and Powys's loved negroes, if educated, would, he says, after a note on the African origins of the Welsh and recalling that Rabelais borrowed his story from the legends about Merlin, be Rabelais' ideal readers (V, 336). Religion is contained. Powys admits the sensitising accomplishment of the Christian era (IX, 398). But just as Paul developed Jesus' personal gospel into assertion of ' the Christ ' *within,* so Rabelais goes further to emphasise more generally 'the unfathomable well-spring of creative power', the ' Christ-quality', in all of us, so making a transference from static theologising to a dynamic psychology (IX, 385-7, 395). Jesus himself used this well-spring; Rabelais is not less than a Christian but more (IX, 386, 393). In his 'mingling of Pauline charity with Homeric laughter' (IX, 392) he offers us a ' Fifth Gospel' (III, 307).

These pages constitute Powys's most explicit statement on his pluralistic philosophy. The Trinity as ruler of a prisoning totalitarian block-universe is rejected in favour of the Pythagorean 'four' and Whitman's ' Square Deific' (VII, 376, 358) — of a multiverse of unsystematised possibilities (VIII, 377). The Aquarian wisdom must be aligned with the feminine principle. Though Rabelais may appear to be an anti-feminist, his humour has in fact exact feminine reference, if only because, since male repellences would not normally trouble the less fastidious outlook of a woman (IV, 327; VII, 358-62), men are being forced by it into the woman's world. Rabelais and Powys are replacing male idealism with a more feminine comprehension.

Rabelais' ' wise, merciful and magnanimous giants' (V, 332) are in line with Powys's habitual interest in, and liking for, giants, from the Cerne Giant onwards. His ' cyclopean excremental and sexual extravagances' (X, 406) are for a purpose; his very grossness is an earth-love, and his religion one of ' unconquerable good-temper, heroic enjoyment, and the worship of the unfathomable mysteries of Nature' (VIII, 373). Such is our Messiah of the Aquarian era (VIII, 374).

Rabelais, like Powys, was fascinated by the occult and ' whatever Dimension of Life lies behind and above our souls' (IX, 393). And yet Powys rejects the word ' spirit', while admitting its power for St Paul whom he so regularly admires, as a Rabelaisian adjunct (IX, 396). Some of the problems posed by the word are faced in the book we turn to next, *In Spite Of* (1953).

In Spite Of involves us in close analysis of what might be called the heart of Powys's doctrine : the power of soul-projection, of which Owen Glendower was a master and of which Powys has already said much.

We are to attempt to make our consciousness embrace, with *all* our senses in play, some *distant* object a few hundred yards away, in a bridal union (IV, 111, 116; IX, 293, 300). The act is described again and again. It is argued that though we shall *feel* independent of the body we are nevertheless using its senses and not so independent as we think; we are attached to it by ' a living stream of vibrating magnetism ', called also an ' elastic ' and yet ' invisible ' ' navel-string ' (IV, 109, 124; VII, 215, 218). This is the silver cord already envisaged in *The Inmates*. During this projection the body itself will be in a state of trance (VII, 204; IX, 299). This extension of consciousness is claimed, in the exact manner claimed by John Davidson for his own closely related teaching in *The Theatocrat* and *The Triumph of Mammon,* to be a racial and evolutionary advance, though it may take many centuries, towards ' a new self-created self ' (IV, 122; V, 130) of utmost importance (IV, 106, 110, 113, 116-7, 122-3; VII, 214-5, 218, 223; VIII, 246; IX, 299, etc). Wordsworth (p. 19) made a similar claim.

Though his descriptions fall in direct line with psychic studies Powys is careful to distinguish them from any attempt at ' verification ' in the cause of ' psychical research ', because what he is counselling is, he says, perfectly natural. It

undermines the whole emotional atmosphere of this imaginary supernatural world which has been spell-binding us for two thousand years

because it is ' in full harmony with Nature '. Psychic studies are accordingly grouped with the Christian tradition as tempting us to a dangerous supernaturalism (IV, 124). The physical body is not affected: ' There is no need to think of a deserted body lying in a trance till the soul returns to it ' (IV, 124). And yet Owen Glendower was regularly in a trance-like state during soul-projection and later in our present study we are told that at such times the body ' will probably stand erect in a blind, deaf, unfeeling, unsmiling, untasting trance ' (IX, 299; and see VII, 204; IX, 293). There is a definite contradiction.

Powys's fear of religion, which he regards as responsible for many cruelties (IX, 278), appears to constrict his thought. Of his present philosophy he writes :

Its attitude to religion resembles the attitude of many active and practical persons towards what is called ' Spiritualism '. It contains an instinctive dread of being led into contact with a whole dimension of strange, unruly, disorderly forces that can be very dangerous to our natural peace of mind and to our normal human activities.

(IV, 94)

But what of Powys's faith elsewhere in the multiverse, in the myriad Whitmanesque dimensions, in the anarchic as a saving principle? When he rejects

those doubtful, plausible, specious, spiritualistic, telepathic, Yogiish, ' successes ' which have done more to confuse and bewilder and side-track people with a nervously alert and sensitive intelligence like ourselves than any traditional belief has ever done,

(IX, 293)

the rejection is pragmatic rather than metaphysical. He tells us that belief in survival is as dangerous as ' supernatural religion ' (IV, 91). He asserts that when we die we are obliterated (VII, 197) and that soul-projection cannot be, though he admits that it seems to be (VIII, 252-3), that of a ' disembodied spirit ', because ' there is no such thing as a disembodied spirit ' (IV, 115); a statement that follows awkwardly the aspersions in *Mortal Strife* (IV, 113) on ' rationalists ' who are so ' simple-minded ' as to suppose death points to nothingness, and the vivid delineation of disembodied spirits in *Morwyn*. In *Mortal Strife* man was regarded as amphibious, already half out of space and time; here we are locked within them. *In Spite Of* is sometimes less dogmatic, as in the non-committal ' before we die and are no more seen ' (VIII, 248), but a confusion remains, the more acute for the assertion of the existence of ' higher ' beings ' in this or in other dimensions as superior to us as we are to reptiles ' (IV, 122). Apparently each has to remain as it is : there is no moving *up*.

Powys's consciousness seems to have plunged so deep and expanded so widely in mastery of space that temporal extension, as we found in his narrative technique (p. 80 above), begins to lose authority. Normally we think of space as within time; in Powys space has begun to swallow time. Insight so reduces egoism that survival becomes an irrelevance; the sky's infinity makes life so marvellous as to be utterly satisfying apart from any thought of it (IV, 91; VIII, 237). Despite his dissatisfaction with modernistic poetry (*Obstinate Cymric*, VIII) his own thought-lines are running parallel to its tendency to concentrate in depth or height on particularities without temporal reference. Such thinking presupposes a state already within a dimension wherein futurity, and therefore all questions of survival, lack meaning; a state, some would call it, of ' eternal life '. Only so can we make sense of Powys's assertion that the ' I ' can feel immune from, and ' outside the radius ' of, even a ' planetary disaster ' (VII, 207).

While however we continue thinking we must allow time some

rights. Our difficulties can only be met by supposing some intermediary between the physical and the spiritual corresponding to the 'psycho-physical' powers (IV, 106) which are under discussion, such as the soul-bodies in *Morwyn* and the cloudy form of The Inmates (pp. 65, 82-3 above). These are the 'etheric' or 'astral' body of spiritualism, the silver cord being severed from the physical at death. This, too, is the solution advanced by St Paul in positing a 'spiritual body' (1 Corinthians XV, 44). Powys rejects the Pauline conception in *Mortal Strife* (V 133), while in effect using it freely in *Morwyn*.

In Spite Of counters *Porius* regarding the male-female nature of the soul, seeing the complete being as bisexually integrated (VII, 222). To such a being a human partner will, though Powys regards sexual companionship as helping the process, be, we may suppose, less sexually relevant; and that may be why we hear that the natural 'bride' or 'bridegroom' of the soul is, as it was for so many 'Powys-heroes', the external, often inanimate, world (IV, 116). More question-able, at least in view of the fearful evils in Powys's own works, is his affirmation of 'the essential goodness of human nature' (VIII, 241). His philosophy is, as usual, regarded as more feminine than masculine, and he pays a tribute to Sibyls and Prophetesses (VIII, 248; IX, 272-4). 'Unravished virgins' are, as elsewhere, regarded as repositories of wisdom (IX, 308).

An important emphasis falls on (i) the ether, or sky, and (ii) poetry. This miraculous air, ether, or sky surrounds the globe as a 'divine' support (II, 45; III, 51). Being 'boundless' (VIII, 235), its spatial *infinity* makes life utterly satisfying whether or not we survive death (VIII, 237). The term 'ether' has a long tradition, Greek, esoteric, and scientific, representing the highest refinement of matter. It may be compared to Powys's described sensation of making matter 'porous' (VII, 199). While rejecting the etheric body as an independent entity, Powys nevertheless regards the etheric as his divine principal. Close to it is poetry. Rabelais' faith was poetic, counselling 'the poetic-humorous way' (*Rabelias*, VIII, 377). *In Spite Of* urges us to replace the supernatural by the poetical, for poetry includes theology (VIII, 231-3; 256-7; IX, 297). It is through the poetic 'sixth sense' that we respond to the mystery of the ether (VIII, 237). It seems that the ether and poetry together are being regarded as even more ultimate than 'the great planetary mother' (VIII, 235) which the ether supports. There is a suggestion of

our pre-human origin in the womb of some zodiacal, etheric, elemental ' Great Mother ', some unutterable *Dona Dea* of our terra-
queous dimension in this infinitely receding multiverse.

(V, 150)

Despite his polytheistic pluralism it seems that Powys has after all
what looks like a central divinity; or at least, if he has one, it will be
the Ether.

We pass now to *Homer and the Aether* (1959). Rabelais offered
' a mingling of Pauline charity with Homeric laughter ' (*Rabelais,*
IX, 392). Powys loves Homer for his humour, polytheism and magical
delight in chaotic events and material objects, but since such a
pluralistic world precludes analysis Powys honours him in two ways :
(i) by retelling the story of the *Iliad* through (ii) the consciousness of
the new goddess, the Ether, regarded as his inspirational helper. The
name ' Aether ' is spelt now in Greek-Roman style. She is defined
by her preliminary address ' The Aether Speaks ' (though my numerals
apply to subsequent references). The Aether is from above our atmosphere which to her has the density of fog (XXIII, 268), but she can
also interpenetrate matter; she is the element within which all creation
floats. She acts through air and fire suffused by her own peculiar light.
Her inspiration is distinguished from the traditional literary qualities
of metric and music, though these have their value and her clairvoyant
realism needs to be supplemented by the poetic imagination (XXIII,
263). What she alone can do is to make Homer understand not only
the mental processes of gods and men but also the kind of semi-
consciousness, derived from human association, of supposedly inanimate objects; and she can awaken him to moral and semi-Christian
valuations (XXII, 261). Sex she understands, and the mystery of
virginity, and can make Homer see into and love those most ordinary
and trivial-seeming activities that were honoured long past by old
Mrs Renshaw in *Rodmoor*. Homer's wisdom is feminine (*In Spite Of,*
VI, 165). Such is Powys's etheric deity existing at the impingement of
mind on matter, immortal beyond all gods and men.

The conclusion to her address is fascinating. Just as Powys's explicit
thought is less at home with human survival than are his imaginative
creations, so he makes his Aether state first the blessedness of death
as an ultimate conclusion and afterwards, for those who want it, she
draws so sweet a picture of Elysian bliss that logic is crowned with an
authority beyond itself :

What I am going to help you to do, you old indomitable, indefatigable Homer of my heart, is to accept and enjoy to the limit all the ordinary events in that human life of yours, which, wherever it is played out, is always a magnified view, or a minimized view, of some kind of Trojan War. Yes, I want to help you to describe the amazing life of mortals upon the earth; and when you have ushered each one of them in turn to the brink of the grave I want you to make them long to lie down in peace and sleep an unbroken sleep, or to soothe them, if they are afraid of annihilation, by lovely dreams of a kindly Hermes-Angel who will guide them gently, softly, swiftly when the end comes, to some blest Elysian Field where they can meet everybody again that they want to meet, and forget everything they want to forget forever and forever and forever.

('The Aether Speaks', 29)

In invoking the Aether Powys has come under her power.

Powys has his own trinity: the Aether as God the Mother; Poetry, as the Son, or perhaps daughter; and Humour, for the spirit, the *Tao*, or 'Way'.

CHAPTER VII

Myths and Marvels

Homer and the Aether comes well within Powys's final period. His last works, though simple in style and lucid in narration, are far from easy. Though the stories seem fanciful, their thought-content is keen and often disturbing. They are as much problem-stories as statements. Powys is submitting his old interests to new critiques. What we expect to be elevated may be, or seem to be, deflated. It is easy to feel lost.

Atlantis (1954), set in the Homeric world, crams more Greek mythology and modern thought into a single narrative than might have seemed possible. Nevertheless the narrative is unimpeded, exerting a forward thrust and keen suspense, leading to a strong climax. Our hero is the young Nisos, son of Odysseus who in old age plans to leave Ithaca, as in Tennyson's *Ulysses,* for a westward voyage over Atlantis, which has been sunk by Zeus. Around, the world, or cosmos, is being shaken by disruptions which have clear contemporary reference for ourselves. The Olympian establishment is threatened by an uprising of two main powers : (i) Titans and giants, formerly either quiescent or harshly controlled and (ii) the feminine principle.

Zeus has lost his thunder, his companions desert him, Pan has joined with the disruptive forces and all order is in danger (I, 32-3; III, 75-95; IV, 104; V, 157-8; VII, 218, 225-6; IX, 330; XI, 383). The dragon-giant Typhon, prisoned under Etna, has broken loose (V, 156; VII, 219, 220-1, 225-6, 239-40). The insurgence of subnormal and supernormal giants of an older order (VII, 217; XI, 391) against established orthodoxy enjoys a natural Powysian sanction. So does the recurring insistence on uprising feminine powers (I, 33; III, 80-1; V, 140-2; VII, 225; IX, 297; XI, 391; and see VI, 178). There is the usual emphasis on maids and old maids as repositories of good (III, 75, 77, 80).

The rising is summed up as an insurrection of old against new gods; it is an insurrection of giant, animal, dragon, serpent and woman gods, for ' the older times were matriarchal times ', in accord with the Earth Mother (VII, 217). We are reminded of ' the Golden Age ' under Kronos,* or Saturn (V, 142), who is said, with presumably a reference to Wales, to be awaiting his awakening in ' Ultima Thule ' (VI, 208); and Crete, the reputed home of the Golden Age, is often referred to (IV, 113; VII, 217, 224, 238; X, 368). The feminine assertion looks back for its authority to Kronos of the Golden Age with his ' Peace to all Beings ' in strong contrast to the ' accursed Olympians ' and their inauguration of competition and conflict (I, 35; VII, 224-5).

Gold is here a dominating impression attaining splendour in the mystic gleams of the golden armour of Achilles placed by Arsinöe the Trojan, daughter of Hector, on the effigy of Hector (I, 30; VIII, 277-81; IX, 282), and in the gold-worship of Zenios (VI, 204-5).

Odysseus' plan is to voyage *over* and *beyond* the sunken Atlantis to the ' Unknown West ' (IV, 118; VI, 208; VII, 222, 229; IX, 298, 310, 330). This is regarded as a high endeavour. Zeus in his extremity unites with Themis (Law) and Atropos (Fate) in deciding that the best thing ' here and now ' — we may suspect a contemporary reference — is for Odysseus to sail towards the ' Isles of the Blessed ' (III, 95; and see XI, 387).

It is natural to associate Atlantis (see p. 74) with Powys's conception of the Golden Age *below* Hell in *Morwyn*. Atlantis has been sunk by Zeus (II, 49-50; IV, 118). The causes are : they would not believe Zeus existed; their inventions were blasphemous; and they were interfering with sexual processes to create a bisexual being, an innovation the Olympians could not stand since ' they have always been extremely touchy and sensitive on such points ' (IX, 330; X, 347; XII, 435; VIII, 260). It reads like a contemporary critique. Remembering Powys's earlier emphasis on some new ' Saturnian ' bisexuality (pp. 25, 60), we tend to favour Atlantis; and it can be associated with Pan, the idyllic garden of the Hesperides and the lost earth-goddess Maia (VII, 219; IX, 294). But there are difficulties. The enemies of Zeus are not all likable. The older animal-deities are repellent to our boy-hero Nisos (XI, 391), and the two ancient goddesses Eurybia and Echidna,† who function as choric presences, are

---

* For this and other names I follow Powys's use of Greek lettering in *Atlantis*.
† For Echidna, see *Porius*, XXVI, 611; for Eurybia, *In Spite Of*, V, 138.

associated with Hell and monsters (I, 26-8; VII, 222-6; IX, 289; XI, 391). The female principle includes Harpies and Furies (III, 80-1, 87-8, 93). The revolutionary powers are of varied and sometimes ambiguous colouring. Kronos and the Golden Age are unquestioned, and the continual designation of him as ' Son of Kronos ' gives Zeus a certain lustre. Other powers are more dubious, and Atlantis itself, which is not to be identified with the Golden Age, we shall find dangerous. Zeus may have been right to sink it.

Odysseus' plan is opposed by Enorches, a fanatical priest of Orpheus, the mystery religions, Dionysos and Eros as against the Olympian deities. Here again we are plunged into ambivalence. He has a ' carrion-crow physiognomy ' (V, 147); he is called ' devilish ', arouses ' disgust ', and his retainers are vulgar and illiterate (IV, 128; III, 97; III, 71). But as an orator his ' demonic personality ' is impressive (VIII, 257), and some people regard him as a saint or angel (XII, 423; VIII, 252). He is ' this terrible priest of *none knew what* ' (III, 98). His primary assertions are the Orphic mysteries, Eros and Dionysos. Orpheus was a poet (III, 96). Eros is deity of self-loss in love, Dionysos of ecstacy through drink. The occult is simultaneously involved (IV, 110; V, 137), and the fear throughout the story that Tartaros has broken loose may hold a reference to modern spiritualism (II, 49-50; V, 158-9, 166; IX, 289). When Enorches claims that his mysteries distil the essence of Hellenism (V, 138) we may, remembering Euripides' deities in the *Hippolytus* and *The Bacchae*, be inclined to agree. He is asserting the power through ecstacy of touching what is beyond normal awareness, Eros for the ' Secret behind life ' and Dionysos for the ' Secret behind Death '; and the two are found to be ' identical ' (V, 143). He regards the Olympian theology as merely childish (V, 136, 143), and in an extended and superb declaration, in which passion is said to be delivered *without any loss of coolness and poise*, he supports Atlantis against the ' curst Olympian rulers ' who sank it, while explaining its bisexual innovations (VIII, 259-60). His own tenets are original; only now, he says, do ' Eros and Dionysos appear in their true light ' (V, 137). His is the ' young Eros of the Mysteries ' who ' can make love to both sexes and be loved by both ', a ' new and different Eros ' from previous conceptions, for Aphrodite has left mortals for her old spouse Hephaistos (V, 157).

Both Enorches and Atlantis are aligned with bisexuality and both are at odds with Olympian convention. Nisos recognises a truth, such as that proclaimed in Aristophanes' *The Birds,* in the doctrine that Eros is the origin of all things (V, 145); though perhaps the coolness and poise with which Enorches delivers his passionate oration, together with the ' new dimensions of being ' he asserts, associates him more nearly with Plato (VIII, 261). Criticism of Enorches is sharp. Love, as Powys so often tells us, brings in hate, and Enorches is called the prophet of both (V, 151). To a sinner his ' priestly authority ' can be ' pompously perverse ' and ' necrophiliastically censorious ' (IX, 290) : we are invited to see in him the dangers of an esoteric wisdom assuming sacerdotal authority. The dangers of Dionysos and Eros are witnessed by their having put Herakles in a state of ecstacy during which he allowed the dragon-giant Typhon to escape (VII, 219, 225). The farmer Zeuks insists that Enorches really hates life — as did Mr Hastings in *Ducdame* — and that his twin deities are simply names for ' Not-Being ' and a plunge into ' Nothingness ' (VI, 183, 192-3; X, 368-9). Enorches eventually goes half-mad and sings a paean to ' Nothing ' (XI, 376-7), but it is suggested that the cause may have been simply the hatred and lack of response he had received (XII, 422). Nisos, whom we trust, realises that the ecstasy he worshipped was ' a real, actual, concrete experience ', and in the new land in the West he is to be allowed a community to preach to (XI, 395-7). He has something in common with Puritanism.

In this ' ambiguous ', ' weird ' and ' disturbing ' (III, 67; XI, 397) figure and his ' Half-Deaths of mystical ecstasy ' (VI, 197), we have a perfect expression of Powys's ambivalent attitude to certain of his own more visionary-mystical experiences. In sex, he has regularly repudiated the Lawrentian mysticism of sex-darkness while concentrating on a diffused and fully conscious approach (e.g. pp. 45, 50, 59); Sylvanus Cobbold asserted the power to be conscious of areas previously subconscious (p. 46); on drink Powys seems never to have philosophised except once in a chapter of *Rodmoor* (XIV, 180-1); and on the spiritualistic-occult he is invariably cautious, and sometimes hostile. Nevertheless, his own experiences have touched each realm, apart from drink. Mysteries he recognises, but what he dislikes is mystery *as a subject of worship* ending up by reducing, instead of enriching, the mystery of life itself (VI, 192-3). To Odysseus Enorches hides a ' spadeful of good turf under bushels of mystical bad hay ' (V, 147).

In *Lucifer* Pan, the earth-deity, received greater poetic approval than Dionysos. In *Atlantis* the part of Pan, who has revolted against his Olympian begetter Hermes (VII, 225-6), is small, but he has a representative in the rough countryman Zeuks, often supposed his son, who stands for a Rabelaisian philosophy in contrast to Enorches' mysticism.

Zeuks is a local Ithacan farmer, not tall but massive, whose appearance expresses deep thought, sensuous enjoyment, an indomitable zest for life and a ' humorous relish for every conceivable aspect of human existence and of animal sensation ' (V, 131; VI, 209). Like Broch-o'-Meifod, of whom he is a humorous successor, he asserts the annihilation of the soul at death (VII, 246), though he can also express doubts of it (VI, 183). He is a rebel against all established authority (IV, 122). His philosophy opposes systems and wars in the name of peaceful activities and the creating of joy from our ' secret selves '. Opposites cannot be fused or mingled; rather must we deal in advances and retreats, steering our way and exerting ' defiance ' against whatever life offers (VI, 180-2). His expression can register a ' formidable ' and ' powerful humour ' (VI, 185). His humour and capacity for enjoyment make him see and even enjoy the limitations of his own philosophy of defiance, of which he has doubts (VI, 209; IX, 284).

In these doubts he is a perfect expression of Powys himself in his present sharp and often humorous critique of his own various directions. The rustic Zeuks, whose life-view is in the main highly approved, nevertheless has to undergo Enorches' slaughterous denunciation :

> Did you think, Dung of the Earth, did you suppose, Turd of the World, that the Stars in their Courses would fight for a blob, a shred, a foul pellet, a filthy crumb, a drop of cuckoo-spit, a clipping of toe-nail, like you?
>
> (V, 135)

Zeuks' status is heightened by his having gained possession of the two semi-divine horses, the winged dark-skinned Pegasus and the whitish grey but black-maned Arion (IV, 113, 127).

A third philosopher is Telemachos, Odysseus' son and priest of Athene, who delivers a truly tremendous discourse expanding the Wordsworthian doctrine (p. 19). We are to *embrace* earth, the heavenly bodies, and the ether beyond, till all become one life, and by the ' inexhaustible power ' in us we shall influence and drive this

' New Enormity ' which we have ' created ', moulding it nearer our ' heart ' :

> Now you may naturally say that you are only one of the innumerable separate individual lives who are working and willing and re-creating and re-moulding this existent one or super-one made of earth-ocean-sun-moon-stars and immeasurable depths of divine ether; and you will be perfectly right in saying this. You *are* only one of the many wills who are driving this earth-ocean-sun-moon-stars and immeasurable depths of ether forward upon its way. *Its way whither?*
>
> Ah! that is the impenetrable secret of which you are yourself a living part and a partial creator. You, a secret agent, have an obscure purpose in your mind; and so have your innumerable fellow-agents driving the universe *on its way;* but on its way *to what* — ah! *that* remains an impenetrable secret!

(VII, 237-8)

Telemachos's features are ' majestic ' and ' severe '. His life has been spent in sea-walks and meditations among parchments inscribed by artists of Sumeria and Crete. He is tired, and can feel a desire to escape from the struggle; on survival he maintains a ' rigid agnosticism ' (VII, 238-9, 246). Athene, goddess of wisdom, is the ' greatest of all Goddesses ', and it might be well if her philosopher-priest, whose position has been of late ' usurped ' by Enorches, and who has himself seen the Dionysian powers without ' wanting to join them ' (IX, 319-20; X, 350; II, 53), would accept the throne when Odysseus leaves (IX, 320). But throughout our narrative Athene, in contempt of human and cosmic confusion, is absent among the Ethiopians whose innocent worship pleases her (IV, 104-5; VI, 207); and a rival claimant obliterates the House of Odysseus (X, 356). The comments are contemporary.

Odysseus is convincingly presented as an old man of wide experience and exact purpose. He is massively broad and his bald head has grandeur. He is like a Titan or a God (II, 45-6). He can always, whatever the situation, dismiss from his mind whatever does not concern his immediate purpose (VI, 188; VII, 246; VIII, 263).

Hitherto Powys-heroes have been mature men of academic interests. In Nisos, a boy approaching seventeen devoted to Odysseus whose son he turns out to be, we have a new type. He cherishes the ambition to be a prophet, not, like previous prophets, for intellectuals such as himself, but rather for the ' strong ' and ' healthy ', who have ' been hurt in some way '. His aim is to think from himself ' outwards '; not like Enorches 'towards himself inwards' (III, 83-4; 98-9). The thought chimes with Powys's interest in the massive and giant-like, and his tendency to rate mysticism below simplicity.

As Odysseus and his friends voyage westward on a ship whose figurehead represents the ruler of sunken Atlantis, we hear more of that ruler's wisdom, recorded pictorially and *spatially* by 'landscape' rather than 'rhythm' (X, 335-6, 339). The figure, scaled, feathered and beyond all precedent intellectual, neither beast, man nor god (X, 341-2, 364), suggests that this 'wicked magician' dominates the voyage (X, 347). The figure's face, if fully seen, is known to strike an appalling horror (XI, 375-6). Eventually Odysseus and Nisos descend into sunken Atlantis. The wondrous city breathes through silence the elemental speech-music of the inanimate, while metaphorically composing, with all its intricacies and edifices, 'one vast musical composition in marble and stone' (XII, 428, 432-3). They find its Ruler, reclined on putrifying sea-weeds, a goddess-titan 'completely bi-sexual and androgynous', of 'shocking' appearance. It exerts on Nisos a mesmeric attraction, gesturing ritualistically to him and Odysseus with horrible claws, offering conquest of the universe. The boy is fascinated by 'the appalling beauty and over-mastering power of the face above those flickering hands and that androgynous breast' (XII, 436-9). Though the 'incalculable Entity' is given the most loathsome leprous and deathly associations (XII, 446-7), Nisos feels that 'to see the terrible beauty of this majestic face' destroyed 'would be to assist at the most savage crime that his wickedest imaginations had ever pictured'. But his deepest 'I am' gives different counsel (XII, 449). When the Thing speaks, its voice is rasping and mechanical; it asserts Science, the utter domination, throughout the centuries, of the will to *know*, irrespective of humane values. Ulysses' club, the club of Herakles, slayer of the Nemean Lion (I, 27), now released from the withholding grasp of son and father, by its own power and volition crashes down, shattering the Horror. Nisos determines to be a prophet against Science (XII, 451-5).

The conception is deliberately ambivalent. The Being's bisexuality recalls the bisexual emphasis and 'Saturnian sex' of the *Autobiography* (p. 60 above); and also Tegolin in *Owen Glendower*. We have already learned that Atlantis aroused Zeus' opposition because of its sexual divagations. Such unity-ideals, in early narratives and again in *Porius* distrusted, are here identified with Powys's worst evil:

scientific cruelty. This seems strange; but we have already established a relation of the sylphic intuition to deep evil (pp. 31-2, 61, 65), and Powys's best magicians such as Uryen Quirm were habitually given deathly and repellent associations. In Atlantis and Enorches, and also in the 'unholy' and yet presiding hell-deities Eurybia and Echidna who would thwart the spring of 'sexual life' and 'pervert' the 'intentions of nature' (I, 28), we have ethically ambiguous conceptions. Zeuks rejected the fusion of opposites (p. 97 above; cp. pp. 80-1).

Though the Atlantean Being's appearance has a 'beauty' and 'power' (XII, 439) recalling the application of those words to the seraphic boys in *Rodmoor* and *Ducdame* (pp. 26, 27), the repetition need scarcely suggest a repudiation of them too. In our hero Nisos a boy is given hero-status, possessing an appeal the more compelling for his sexual innocence (XII, 412), prophetic aims and youthful dreams, as when on the midnight sea he cries to his unknown soul-mate:

Are you a lonely girl who want me for your mate? Or are you a lonely boy who want me for your 'Hetairos' or friend? Speak, you Mystery of the Night! Speak and tell me which of the two you are!
(XI, 386)

Odysseus and Nisos visit, but are not subdued by, Atlantis; Atlantis is not, though it has affinities to, the Golden Age, and our heroes are now looking not past, but forward. The Saturnian quest always involved a *descent* that may be, or seem, dangerous. In Atlantis and Enorches Powys presents good-evil Powysian complexes deliberately tilted *down*, as in Christie Malakite, Uryen Quirm and Myrddin Wyllt, who are all given repellent connotations, they are tilted *up*. In *Morwyn* we had to descend *below* Hell to find Saturn; here our descent is a brief visit only, and we next travel on, above the terror, for new lands. Our balance favours the Rabelaisian Zeuks, the practical Odysseus, and the untainted boy-hero Nisos. Ajax, just before dying, tells Zeuks, who is beside him, of a mysterious and bottomless hole, where some see darkness and some light, and he had always dreamed 'of meeting a laughing man at the bottom of that hole' (VIII, 279). In this passage Zeuks' humorous wisdom itself assumes depth as the golden prize, beyond darkness.

Giants are in conflict with gods, and nothing in *Atlantis* is more superbly imagined than the two giants, Nimrod the Hunter and the escaped dragon-giant Typhon, raging beneath ocean in mutual conflict. We are in a world of living myth. The divine steed Pegasus, exquisitely realised in both animality and divinity, serves to crown the succession of earlier horses, the ' godlike ' stallions of the Horse-Fair in *Wolf Solent* (IX, 184 or 172), Wizzie Ravelton's old circus horse, Rhisiart's sturdy pie-bald, Tegolin's grey charger, and the great mare of *Porius;* all are retrospectively honoured in Pegasus. The mythical feeling, by which a tree can have its wise Dryad, is an off-shoot of Powys's consistent recognition of consciousness on all creation's levels. Most vivid of all are the recurring dialogues, male with female, of the intellectual fly Myos and the mystical moth, Pyraust, summing all Powys's love of insects. In *Atlantis* as elsewhere girls in mutual conversation are brilliantly realised and there are many important women, divine and human; but there is the usual lack of feminine characterisation accompanying the equally usual assertion, and even dominance, of the female principle. There is however one exception to this weakness, if weakness it be : Pyraust. The girl-moth is probably more of an individual girl, or woman, than any of the divine or human people. Such is the power of Powys's self-identification with the non-human. Nor is it confined to life-forms : there is the recurring telepathic conversation between the oracular Sixth Pillar of Odysseus' palace in Ithaca and the Club of Herakles, functioning even when the Club is in mid-Atlantic, like wireless telegraphy, just as Pegasus brings people out to the ship like an aeroplane and Odysseus' Helmet of Proteus serves as a diver's apparatus when he and Nisos descend into ocean.

Nothing in our literature bears any resemblance to this unique fusion of ancient myth and contemporary thought. It is the most intricately patterned of all Powys's books; and it is both difficult and disturbing. But though its most intense conceptions are the ambivalent and esoteric powers, the spirit of the handling is nearer to the spirit of Zeuks, whose name recalls Zeus and who, despite all tragic sympathies, dies laughing (IV, 112; XII, 461-2). Humour is here a rival and unvanquished deity. Matching our golden impressions we have a subtle and golden humour strong throughout, including the many verbal extravagances of contumacious rhetoric. There is also, throughout, in correspondence to the white marble and blue sea and the sun-path on the waters of our setting, a sweetness and a serenity carried in a prose as lucid as a mountain stream, breathing, as from its hero Nisos, a purity and youth looking not to a lost past, but forward. Enorches stands for a valid mysticism but a mysticism gone mad;

Athene and her priest Telemachos might have saved the situation, but it is too late. Atlantis with its bisexual penetrations stands for human idealism and advance gone wickedly astray and so in all its splendour and its intellect and its wickedness for ever sunk. Kronos is of the forgotten past. In Zeuks and Nisos, who are together at the end, we have intimations of a different gold.

Atlantis was forecast by the early *Lucifer* (pp. 17-18). Lucifer rejected oriental religions for the Fortunate Isles in the Atlantic whereon he would found his Cosmopolis on Hope, Joy and Youth (IV, 111-2).

The Brazen Head (1956), which opens in an ' ancient circle of Druidic stones ' (I, 9), returns us to Dorset in the thirteenth century when Friar Roger Bacon was working on the invention of a metallic Head able to speak oracles. We have, again, a young hero, John, son of Sir Mort Abyssum and a devoted disciple of Friar Bacon. Evil is represented, not very vividly, by Baron Maldung of ' Lost Towers ', an edifice of black stone that might have come from prehistoric Atlantis (VIII, 112). Maldung's retainers are uniformed in a sickly red.

Sir Mort imagines his soul as a spear thrusting deep into earth or shooting among the stars and thence into an exquisite ' music of nothingness ' (III, 52-4). He believes in an invisible dimension where ' sense-emanations ' and ' thought-eidola ' from all creation exist for a while as entities, but despite his fears of personal extinction he does not believe in full personal survival (IV, 165-6). His second son John, past eighteen but looking younger (X, 140), is sexually inexperienced; he adores girls but his imagination always forces a premature orgasm precluding a satisfactory union (X, 141). He is a free-thinker and has theological arguments with his orthodox elder brother who is making a shrine for the Virgin.

Friar Bacon has by ecclesiastical authority been confined to Bumset Priory for his impious researches, heretical tendencies and addiction to heathen books; but he remains a sound Trinitarian (XIV, 219). He has vision and can envisage the rational soul as a fiery man-god informing and yet independant of the physical body (VI, 84). Whether his brass Head contains a spark of the Holy Spirit is doubtful; it seems nearer modern science (XX, 286; XVIII, 265; XXII, 347); he admits to being mastered by a force independent of *either* God *or* Devil that promises some new revelation (XIV, 210). In order to infuse life into the Head, though he would have preferred an old maid (VI,

81), he gets the Jewish virgin Ghosta to bestride it with her sexual parts in naked contact against its metal (VII, 92, 97; XIII, 207; XIV, 210-1), his scheme giving the recurrent Powysian belief in virgins as a source of revelatory and visionary power a newly concrete expression. It is a kind of ' Parthenogesis ' (XIV, 211).

Theological disquisition is well deployed. The fanatical Bonaventura is an ambitious and self-seeking cleric comically convinced of his personal alliance with God, and apostle simultaneously of love and persecution. He allies himself with Lost Towers against Bacon; the Head is stolen, but recaptured and housed in Sir Mort's armoury. Though Bonaventura is easily obsessed by sexual lust he has the strange capacity of enjoying temptation more than fruition (IX, 119). He is composed as a part-comic satire on orthodoxy at its inquisitorial and casuistical extreme.

More likable is the great Albertus, tutor of Thomas Aquinas. For him the greatest of all achievements by human reason is the philosophy of Aristotle which asserts that nature houses a self-creative energy. This, he recognises, leaves no place for a creator-God; but he nevertheless, through faith, accepts the incompatible philosophy of revelation (XVII, 252-5). We have two choices :

> First the view offered us by the greatest of all human thinkers that the world never had a beginning, but has always existed, and secondly the revelation of Jesus that He and He only is the true Son of God, and that in the beginning God created the world.
>
> (XVII, 257)

Albertus is honest : the two views are presented and his acceptance of the second stated without prevarication. Bacon's attempt to release life from the inanimate he regards as a derivative from Aristotle's principle of energy-in-matter; he himself, aware of this mental driving-force in creation, which he only very diffidently relates to the divine spirit, once started a similar experiment (XVII, 251). He decides to sleep in the Armoury beside the Head.

Beneath his brilliant intellect lies a realm, we are told, of unassimilated and repressed, serpent-like horror, indicating the limitations of his attempt to dominate the pagan by the Christian; and during this night it breaks loose. Between him and the Head hovers the ' blood-stained ' word ' Parthenogesis ' which he had seen inscribed on a near-by figure of the Virgin, and he thinks that the Head has no power over him because ' what your man-maker forgot when he wound you up was the touch of a Virgin '. But he is, as we know, wrong : Bacon's virgin-impregnated Head corresponds closely to Albertus' own total, pagan-Christian, self. That is why

> the imprisoned demonic power in the Brazen Head, which seemed only to have been waiting an opportunity to escape, burst forth to meet what the other was giving.
>
> (XVIII, 270)

Albertus feels himself surrounded by Aristotle's matter, a ' blackish-greyish ' universal and all-basic substance; his own material body expands; and he is borne up into an infinitude of Space. From this nightmare he is rescued by thought of Time and all its familiar and subsuming inclusiveness. The blood-stained word Parthenogesis hovers again between him and the Head. Christ's blood-sacrifice, virginity, and Time are attacked by the repressed horror, Aristotelian matter, and Space. The Head can release this whole conflict, which corresponds to Albertus' whole, pagan and Christian, self, because it has itself been virgin-impregnated. Without that the Head would have had no affect on Albertus.

Our most complex person is Peter Peregrinus, a soldier of fortune and student of imagination. Bonaventura is at the extreme of orthodoxy; Bacon, Albertus and the Head are at a point of balance between orthodoxy and paganism. Peregrinus is wholly hostile to Christianity and sees himself as ' Antichrist ' (XVI, 243).

He has an enormous head dwarfing his body, corpse-white skin, coarse jet-black hair and volcanic eyes (XV, 226-7). He in part recalls Uryen Quirm and Morsimmon Esty. He has, *touching his sexual organs,* a seven-inch pinkish-grey magnet, one end like a head (XXI, 304), with which he aims to, and indeed can, dominate the minds and souls of others and even affect events. The pursuit is a ' mania ' to be contrasted with Bacon's more purely scientific experiments (XVI, 239). Peregrinus is utterly hostile to Bonaventura, thinks Bacon's theological labours foolish, and regards Albertus, in view of his Aristotelian contacts with the secret of matter, as his most dangerous enemy ' among the righteous '; and he himself follows Aristotle in believing that the creative energy of matter has no beginning (XX, 286; XVI, 233-4; XIX, 277; XX, 287).

He is dangerous. A ' devilish power ' might well conclude that no one on earth threatened such harm to the human race as he. The lodestone is called ' demonic ' and his accents when he talks lovingly to his ' Little Pretty ' are sinister (XIX, 273; XXI, 307; XXI, 305).

He can employ his powers to appalling purpose: having witnessed an action of cruelty by Prince Edward he deliberately uses them to assure his son's, that is Edward II's, future death in agony (XIX, 281-2; XX, 295-6). Here Peregrinus is, it is true, acting as an agent of judgment, and his destructive powers have their rationalisations. The human race and all its ways he hates. Had he world-power he would replace the Christian hypocrisy of ' love ' by emphasis on the ' unique self ' in everything; he would ' create a new race of beings altogether, creatures as superior to what mankind is now as man is superior to beasts, birds and fishes ' (XVI, 243). The ' demonic delight ' of these Nietzschean thoughts transports him ' as if in a chariot of air and fire ' that

> flew upward upon the waving of two wings, one of which might have been Space and the other Time, for both together seemed to acquire a mysterious force that soon carried their voyager into a sleep, if sleep it were, where he found himself in reality, if reality it were, beyond all description by the words the human race has hitherto used.
>
> (XVI, 244)

The contesting terms of Albertus' experience, Space and Time, act *together* within Peregrinus' more inclusive ecstacy. As against the Christian emphasis on virginity, represented by the Virgin image and Bacon's use of Ghosta, Peregrinus' magic is sexually virile. His own male organs are part of it. When in the chapter ' The Cerne Giant ' he enjoys sexual union with the seductive Lilith of ' Lost Towers ' on the phallic Giant's hill, he has a Lawrentian experience of creative totality dwarfing the Christian mysteries of Virginity and Jesus' blood with ' the greater Mystery of Procreation ' (XX, 290). Later he tries, for his purposes, to magnetise young John into sexual union with Lilith (XXI, 305). He sees himself as a sexual Antichrist ' destined by the creative power of Nature herself ' to destroy all belief in the Trinity (XXII, 325).

Though Peregrinus is given every possible association of sinister evil, yet he contains much of Powys's cherished thought. Not only the Cerne Giant but Wales also is involved. He stays with Mother Wurzel in a locality which once belonged to an ancient Welsh god or king, Llyr (XX, 284). Sir Mort indirectly associates occultism such as his with the dangers of Welsh invaders (XVI, 236). His ambition is a kind of Grail quest (XVI, 239); to Bacon he seems to be reducing all existence to the Welsh ' *Diddym* ' or ' ultimate void ' (XVI, 239);

and his lodestone is both the ' Wand of Merlin the Brython ' and ' the
Rod of Moses the Israelite' (XIX, 278). Though we are told that
compared with Bacon's ' authentic inventive genius ' Peregrinus' skill
comes from his ' exalted imagination ' only, yet Bacon himself admits
that Peregrinus' ' inspiration ' preceded and even conditioned his own
' invention ' (XXI, 305; XV, 222); rather as alchemy led on to
Renaissance science. Whatever we may think of them we are
reminded that Jesus and Paul would have taken his powers seriouslv
(XIX, 278). People here have cause to. His stone is able to throw
Bacon into a faint, or trance (XV, 228; XVI, 235). Moreover.
whereas Bacon has to submit to his Head being stolen by Lost Towers,
Peregrinus' lodestone in Lilith's hands is, at the book's conclusion. used
to destroy Lost Towers before the lovers together turn it suicidallv
against themselves till they become one ' fiery ball ' of dazzling light
which falls on and destroys the Brazen Head. Before its destruction
the Head, in part following the words which it uses in Robert
Greene's *Friar Bacon* and *Friar Bungay,* attains speech, pronouncing :
' Time *was* ', ' Time *is* ', ' And time *will* — '(XXII, 347-8). The Head
is semi-Christian and semi-scientific. Its failure to complete its final
phrase marks a doubt as to its future authority. The Christian-
theological and thence scientific side of our opposition is vanquished
by our sexual Antichrist of Welsh affinities and occult powers.

Peregrinus is composed of a complex similar to those we found
in *Atlantis* — both Enorches and the Atlanteans were students of
magnetism (*Atlantis,* VIII, 260) — but here matters are simplified
by the heavy stress on the sexual powers. Among our most memorable
events is the reunion and sexual consummation of the Jewish-
Mongolian giant Peleg and the Jewess Ghosta in a cave of ancient
Welsh associations (X, 144; XX, 291). But the relation of the sexual
centres to a dynamic occultism is *The Brazen Head's* main contribution. Sex-power dominates, as well in the virgin Ghosta's impregnation
of the Head as in Peregrinus' phallic lodestone. However a distinction
is apparent in the opposition between Aristotle, paganism and
male-female sexuality against Trinitarian doctrine, Christian blood-
sacrifice and virgin sexuality. Space is on the one side, Time on the
other. Points of contact are in the Brazen Head and John's view
of the Mother as making the Trinity a ' Pythagorean square ' (XXI,
300; and see V, 74; X, 152). Though the stronger power, a kind of
Cerne Giant power, is on the pagan side, it is continually given through

its representative Peregrinus the most sinister associations, and this sinister emphasis is symbolically underlined when near the Welsh cave a voice as from a child of an ancient giant-race buried some million of years ago utters a defiance against both the sun and all future religions, using the refrain 'Penglog y Baban yr Gawr' (the words mean 'skull', 'baby' and 'giant'):

> Until I'm dust I'll enjoy my hour —
>   Penglog y Baban yr Gawr!
> I'll gather my harvest and grind my flour —
>   Penglog y Baban yr Gawr!
> With Holy Rood I'll have nought to do —
>   Penglog y Baban yr Gawr!
> Adam am I and Eve are you,
> And Eden's wherever we are, we two —
>   Penglog y Baban yr Gawr!
> A mortal's fate is the same as a mole's —
>   Penglog y Baban yr Gawr!
> The same as the fishes that leap in shoals,
>   Penglog y Baban yr Gawr!
> Where leaf do fall — there let leaf rest —
> Where no Grail be there be no quest —
> Be'ee good, be'ee bad, be'ee damned, be'ee blest —
> Be'ee North, be'ee South, be'ee East, be'ee West
> The whole of Existence is naught but a jest —
>   Penglog y Baban yr Gawr!

(XVII, 247)

Though the lines mark an acceptance, they remain sinister; there is no sun-warmth nor overtone of humour. In them Powys expresses with grim exactitude the implications of his darker compulsions.

CHAPTER VIII
Fantasy

Sir Mort, Albertus and Peregrinus all experienced sensations of upward flight; and Powys's remaining narratives, neatly accompanied by the metaphysic of *Homer and the Aether* in 1959, are constructed around various sorts of space-adventure. A contrast of Space and Time was forced by our discussion of *Porius* and *In Spite Of,* and is written into *Atlantis* and *The Brazen Head* (pp. 80, 89, 99, 104 above). Space is for Powys the higher category and becomes henceforward an elemental protagonist. In the volume *Up and Out* (1957) we have two stories : *Up and Out* itself and *The Mountains of the Moon.* The first is a satire on orthodoxy and time; the second is more richly compacted, and honours space.

In *Up and Out* our hero, of the earlier Powys-hero type, is named, Gog Goginog and is of Welsh birth. He and his companion the girl Rhitha find themselves on a fragment of earth swimming in space following the destruction of the world by a nuclear explosion. With these are Org, a well-meaning and 'multi-formed' (58) monster developed by the horrors of a vivisectional experiment into a blend of land and sea life that simultaneously serves to make him a universal symbol. He too has his girl, Asm. The four, led by Gog, decide to renounce life in the name of suffering creation.

They see Time as 'an enormous black slug' (35), and when their earth-raft severs it the act symbolises the superiority of substance over an abstraction. Next Eternity appears as a wholly repellent thing which proceeds to swallow the pieces of Time and finally turns inside out, swallowing itself, till nothing remains. Time is shown as weak and eternity as a horrible and factitious invention of religion responsible for untold evil, always trying to turn realities into nothings, voracious, self-contradictory, and finally gone (37-47).

Visitors arrive, including Moloch whom Rhitha had earlier seen trying to devour the Moon (17, 27, 34, 66); and also deities Greek and Welsh, among them Cronos and the gentle Kwang-Tze and humour-

108

less Buddha. Self-destruction is our problem and the star Arcturus comes to announce that the stellar hosts have chosen universal suicide to leave space clean from the horrors of creation (58). The earth-raft and its four occupants are now alone within the ' infinite endlessness ' of ' the tastless, colourless, impalpable, viewless, scentless, indefinable presence of boundless space ' (71, 79).

However, two more persons appear : God and the Devil, the latter conceived, as in Goethe's *Faust,* as the opposer of God's creation. We hear that Space was antecedent to God, who just found himself there, saw the Devil, and saw also particles which could be moulded. Creation has nevertheless proved unsatisfactory. Whether his unhappy creatures survive their death he is not himself sure, and he thinks of starting a new creation avoiding the voracities of nature, with-holding free-will, and assuring everlivingness for all creatures high or low. Gog suggests instead that there may be another dimension altogether and proposes that all six leap into it. Though unsure of its existence, God agrees, and they all take the plunge.

What they find is a mysterious world wherein a beautiful, goddess-like, presence is felt and speech is for a short while telepathic, though all soon becomes a dark sea of nothingness which means complete death. The story reflects Powys's dissatisfaction with traditional theology and metaphysics. It is not all pessimistic; the earth-raft bears up bravely, refusing surrender to the negatives, and Space itself retains honour. The treatment is light and God so happily characterised that satire dissolves into humour.

Inevitably *Up and Out,* by the very nature of its thesis, suffers from a certain emptiness. In contrast *The Mountains of the Moon* is a little gold mine. The title and setting follow the tradition of Dryden's lines, spoken by the Ghost of the hero's mother, in *The Conquest of Granada* :

> Far hence, upon the Mountains of the Moon,
> Is my abode, where heaven and nature smile,
> And strew with flowers the secret bed of Nile.
> Bless'd souls are there refined, and made more bright,
> And, in the shades of heaven, prepared for light.
>
> (Part 2; IV. iii)

Our story is of the real moon-mountains, but many of its associations conform. We hear that these mountains are known by earthly sages as ' The Mountains of Illusion ' (144), representing perhaps a half-way stage of spirit-progress, like the dream-states envisaged in *The Inmates* (p. 84 above) or the 'Bardo' of W. Y. Evans-Wentz's *The Tibetan Book of the Dead*.

Powys's Moon appears to be thinly populated, but its few people are fascinating. Our new hero Rorlt is again a youth, like Nisos and John, scion of an ancient moon-family. He is dangerously fascinated by his beautiful sister Lorlt (137), and climbs the mountains to save her from her lover, Yoom, of whom he is jealous. However he finds instead a lover for himself.

Yoom's father Oom is a sinister being eight feet tall with a head of 'colossal proportions' whose craggy contours suggest a Titan-mountain upthrust from 'unplumbed depths' (143). He lives in the bowels of the Moon, where Rorlt and his father visit him. From there Rorlt starts on his *upward* quest into the mountains, to save his sister.

That the Moon bears a relation to earthly events is witnessed by Oom's collection of 'terrestrial milestones' such as a fragment of the Ten Commandments, the heel of Achilles, one of Nero's fiddle strings, the core of the controversial apple of Eden and a white Feather from the Dove of Noah's Ark (*Genesis* VIII, 8-11). They are vital entities and execute a dance devised according to the Square Deific of Whitman's philosophy (159); and they can even be, as a pack, fierce. The most interesting is the female White Feather felt as ' flitting back to the Ark of Noah, all quivery-fluttery with the sense of duty well over ' (157). She rescues from a cleft a male Black Feather from the Raven of *Genesis* (164-7; *Genesis* VIII, 7), their reunion being as a reunion of long-parted lovers; and this reunion of *white* with *black* we shall find important. A heron's feather, used by Christie Malakite as a book-marker in her copy of Sir Thomas Browne's *Urn Burial,* was a strong symbol in *Wolf Solent* (V, 90 or 81; VIII, 181-2 or 169-70; IX, 210 or 197; 213 or 200; XX, 459-61 or 437-9). The White and Black Feathers and their talk are, in the manner of the Moth and Fly in *Atlantis,* vividly individualised and humanly convincing without for a moment ceasing to be feathers.

Other persons are a scholarly old spinster, Miss Os; a philosopher Om; and the spirit of a Welsh lady who visits the Moon when astral travelling in sleep. We have too an impressive semi-giant, the Hercu-lean Woom-o-Rim, the Moon's son, whose limbs radiate a moon-silvery light and who claims that his father is Mars and not that ' bloated ball of bonfires ' the Sun, to avoid whose lust the Moon had to hide her 'magnetic' and 'magical body'. The Sun he regards as brainless, soulless and heartless (172-6). Woom-o-Rim's opposition to the Sun recalls Uryen Quirm's; his Martial claims make him a symbol of the heroic on a pre-idealistic, Titanic, level.

There are extended philosophical discussions, mostly about Space, which Rorlt says is not empty but 'an enormous living thing' on which our thoughts are impressed (149). The White Feather asserts that all stellar bodies have, like the Moon, an unknown side, looking out into infinitude, and talks of the urge in all of us to escape our prison (171). The philosopher Om is concerned about the relation of Space to the human 'self'. Would Space have any consciousness without this inward — and therefore unspatial — self? Presumably not. A conscious observer appears to be necessary. What is the 'I' of Space? If it be ultimately nothing, then: 'All that exists must exist in something that is nothing. I am the nothing in which everything exists'. He next tries to think himself outside the spatial universe. Everything, even atoms, have *two sides,* one looking outwards and the other inwards. And yet we should not like there to be no mystery about space. Space with an adamantine limit and a self ending in nothingness would be worse than a solid self faced by an unthinkable infinitude (183-5).

Om talks to Yoom and Lorlt who have been making love on the Mountains of Illusion. He insists that Kant was wrong to give Time a status equivalent to that of Space. We have over-emphasised the human at the expense of the cosmic and the material. After all, our existence is dominated not by Time but by the simple compulsions of 'daily labour'. We should copy the enduring 'submissiveness' of the Inanimate and the more we so attune ourselves the more things will conform to what the greatest sages have taught. These thoughts are appropriately accompanied by the antics of a dislodged stone composed of 'reddish manganese' and 'glittering quartz' as it bounds 'ecstatically' down a slope (192-5).

The moon-dwellers' wisdom, he says, is based on 'knowledge', and that of earth-dwellers on what they call 'reason'. While they argue

> we just simply know, and act accordingly; and *that,* with us, is the end of it! And as to our *method* compared with theirs, *theirs* is all *machinery,* whereas *ours* is all *magnetism.*

(216)

The Moon here seems to correspond to what a spiritualist would call the ' etheric ' plane. The passage throws back a certain approval on the dangerous magnetic experiments of *Atlantis* and Peter Peregrinus. Magnetism is an essential property of the Moon (174, 214, 216).

Om is less assured regarding death, talking of the ' strange superstitious terror ' that moon-dwellers themselves have regarding the *other side* of the Moon's mountainous ridge. Rumours exist of tormented souls from earth being cured there; in, as it were, a coalescence of hell and sanatorium. Whether the terror is justified or not he, following Powys's consistent advice regarding death, which is contradicted by his consistent practice, says that it is wiser not to think about the matter. Of survival he concludes that it ' will be as your ideas and thoughts about it create it ', for each creature ' creates ', making his own universe, and these universes ' interlock and intertwine and melt into one another '. The supposed objectivity of earthly science and their gadgets is a mechanically fabricated illusion. Time is of a lesser order than space being a ' human invention ', whereas space is known to every insect (217-9).

We are retravelling ground already surveyed in *Obstinate Cymric* which discussed the reservoirs of power rising from the darkness *at the back of* our minds, though it was also asserted that that darkness was a nothingness (pp. 75-6 above). Elsewhere Plato had his ' Back-of-the-World ' archetypes (*The Art of Happiness;* II, 67); to Sylvanus Cobbold death was ' the other side of life ', and Uryen Quirm deliberately countered No-man's scepticism by comparing the otherness to the ' other side ' of the Moon (pp. 45, 54; *Jobber Skald,* VIII, 264; *Maiden Castle,* VI, 221; and see *Ducdame,* ' moon ', I, 13; also ' behind life ', *A Glastonbury Romance,* XXVII, 935 or 895; *Maiden Castle,* IX, 484; also ' behind ', p. 87 above).

Om begins to weary and even embarrass the lovers Yoom and Lorlt, who have better things on hand than philosophy; and so has Rorlt. For, in contrast to Om's valid yet inconclusive thinking, Rorlt is to climb up, in actuality, to the dividing ridge. The contrast here of thought and action (219) is reflected into what Powys once (p. 62) called the ' cubic ' dimension of fictional statement, whereby the story holds more truth than the thinking.

Rorlt's progress is as follows. He has first penetrated into the Moon's depths to face the sinister giant, Oom. He has come out and up and started to *climb,* in order to save his sister from Yoom. With his club Blob he first resists and next assists the handsome and not unlikable moon-giant Woom-o-Rim. Finding that Yoom and Lorlt are enjoying a genuine love he recognises the wrongness of his fraternal suspicions and jealousy. Rorlt accordingly passes on, and up. Boy though he is, he yet symbolises genius first opposed by and next allied to an aboriginal giant, and affected by yet resisting a dangerous love. He is aware of a procession and a soul music symbolising the tragic harmonies of creation, but knows that it is something that he must ' leave behind ' (207-8). He expects wonders of infinitude beyond the mountain range or rim, and hears a girl's voice from the other side of the moon-ridge (210). At this moment his club Blob assumes control, as the nameless ' will ' assumed control at the moment of Wolf Solent's testing and the club of Herakles took over when the ruler of Atlantis had to be slain. Powys himself and Powys-heroes always had their heavy stick, which served as an animated spirit-companion (*Autobiography,* XII, 644). In *Atlantis* and here it is a club; both clubs have telepathic attributes, and both become con-trolling powers. So led, Rorlt sees the external universe *beyond the rim,* and becomes himself both moon and sky; but even so this super-Wordsworthian union remains only ' half himself ', the other half being the girl whose voice he heard (211), and who has been living alone on the other side of the Moon, tended by the astral travelling soul of the Welsh lady (220). They meet; in union with Helia, daughter of Sun and Moon, Rorlt attains ' a death-in-life ' and ' a life-in-death ' through which

> a new being came into existence who was neither a new boy nor a new girl, but was a fresh experience of that *energeia-akinesis,* or ' energy without agitation ', that in the multiplicity of life's experiences is what really makes for us the blessedness of the un-known future.
>
> (214)

It is as a union of life and death, already hinted by the reunion of the White and Black Feathers. The ' *energeia akinesis* ' is the Aristotelian principle discussed by Albertus in *The Brazen Head.*

This is no normal union : the normal lovers have been left behind on the ' Mountains of Illusion ' (144). Nor is it an unholy love — incest has been repudiated; nor is it a simple Wordsworthianism how-ever vast — that was only half the truth; nor is there any subservience to Titans or giants — Woom-o-Rim was opposed before being assisted;

nor is it some Saturnian gold in the depths — the Moon's bowels have been left for an ascent. Even the faithful club, Blob, descendant of many companion sticks and the club of *Atlantis*, has tumbled down on the *near* side of the ridge. All have played their parts, but the final end, fulfilling Nisos' cry for a soul-mate, criss-crossing the usual sexual associations of Sun and Moon and perhaps indirectly related to the discussions between Rorlt and his sister on bisexuality (140), is the union of a moon-boy with a sun-girl who comes from the Moon's *other*, dark and superstitiously feared, half. Our golden achievement, despite Uryen Quirm, exists through a supernal sex-union in descent from the Sun, whose daughter comes from what had *seemed* the abyss. We are not so very far from *Morwyn*, after all.

Our last two stories pose Powys's basic problem: is our universal key to be a negative or a positive? In both *Rodmoor* and *Ducdame* we heard of books being composed on destruction as creation's heart and end, though in the first this ultimate nothing was a name for ' what lies beyond life ' (XXI, 325) and held a mysterious sweetness. In contrast Sylvanus Cobbold's Absolute declared that It was all that exists and that outside that ' all ' was ' nothing ' (*Jobber Skald*, XI, 428; see p. 46). Continually Powys's thought returns to these vast and simple categories: the last words of *A Glastonbury Romance* are ' Never or Always '. On human survival especially the ambiguity impinges: in *Mortal Strife* we were assured that the otherness beyond sense-perception was the ' extreme opposite of Nothingness ' (VIII, 136), but elsewhere scepticism may be strong. The most expanded discussion comes in the essay on Whitman in *The Pleasures of Literature* where, in attacking the rationalists' denial of other dimensions, Powys imagines their supposed universe before man awoke to consciousness enduring aeons on aeons, millions and trillions of time, with *no observer*:

> There has been, in fact, for these unthinkable immensities — if immensities are to be taken literally as well as mathematically — simply *nothing;* nothing but blind, dark, amorphous matter, nothing but the meaningless and purposeless gyrations of inorganic motion.
> (*The Pleasures of Literature*, 1938; 448)

The passage was unfortunately excluded from the American text in *Enjoyment of Literature*.

All or Nothing (1960) is about creation, space, and nothing. There is often expressed the desirability of filling all space with life-forms (IX, 66; XI, 81; XV, 114; XXI, 155). But there is a negative principle, always willing the opposite. It is as a contrast of Heaven and Hell (XV, 114); and yet, if either side won, existence would be drained of meaning (XVII, 128). Central to the problem is, as before, Space. On Space Powys's thought is driven back as, despite all sceptical questionings, the one irrefragable fact. Is it real? Is it itself creative? Is it conscious?

Earlier stories have introduced us to young hcrocs and space-adventures. Here our young hero has three young companions in a story-world like that of a nursery fairy-tale; and space-adventures are unimpeded and unlimited. We are first in the Dorset area, near Cerne Abbas and Weymouth. John o' Dreams, the hero, has a twin sister Jilly and these eventually pair off respectively with Ting and Ring, children of their neighbour, the prehistoric-looking and hideous giant Lord Urk Cad, hater of the Sun and the human race, who would destroy ' Everything for the benefit of Nothing ' (IV, 31). Presiding over the story are Bubble and Squeak, the one looking like a petrified flower-bowl and the other like a fossilized skull; in the one falling watcr-drops make bubbles that burst to nothing and on the other blobs of earth are raising a pillar. The Skull is that of one of the earliest men. They respectively represent ' Nothingness ' and ' Everything '; one is ' Lady Nothing ', the other ' All There Is ' (VI, 40, 47). As the bubbles burst, the Skull, in opposition, squeaks. However water is certainly the creative origin : the Skull-man himself came from the sea (VI, 41, 47; VII, 56; and see 50). In the first space-adventure Bubblc is a necessary assistant (VIII, 60).

' Squeak ' may be related to the traditional conception of ghosts as squeaking or gibbering. Like a spirit, he uses the hearer's own mind to register his squeak (III, 24). He also explains the nature of ' auras ' and tells John o' Dreams that he and Bubble will come as ' auras ', or spirit-bodies, on their voyage to the Sun (VIII, 60-2). We elsewhere hear that auras are perpetually active around us, and this is true whatever our sceptical intelligences make of it (X, 77). Thoughts hover, like creatures (VII, 55); other dimensions impinge on us (VI, 46); sound is sensed as energy (XIV, 109). The colours they see on the star Vindex are such as no earthly experience has known (XVII, 128), and in it is a city founded on white marble with blazing lights of every colour and emerald walls (XIII, 92-3). A dream, Lorm, is a character here, bisexually imagined (XX, 150). Through the fairy-story the spirit-dimension is often apparent.

We also have some theology. The local priest is in trouble from his bishop for accepting the Son and Holy Spirit but regarding the Father as ' Nothing ' (V, 39; VII, 49). He follows Albertus of *The Brazen Head* in regarding creation as self-creative (VII, 50). God actually speaks to John o' Dreams through a newt, and when asked whether he sides with Bubble or Squeak in his ' private thoughts ' answers :

I am glad you said *private,* for that makes it much easier to explain.
For in my private thoughts I agree with Bubble, but in the thought
I want to have and feel I ought to have, and try to have, I agree
with Squeak.

(XXI, 154)

Afterwards, as a cockroach, when asked which principle will win, God seems about to confess ignorance when he is interrupted (XXII, 162).

Mingling with these mysteries we have a usual down-to-earth Powysian assortment, including Druids, giants, and reminders of Cronos and female deities or rulers (XX, 145). The hero is, as usual, ill-at-ease with crude sexual activity, and like Rorlt loves his own sister almost more than Ting. There is a recurring emphasis on eating : ' we ought to get the sensation of eating and digesting from every single thing we look at ' (VII, 53).

There are three space-adventures. First John o' Dreams descends with Squeak's aura into earth where they solicit help from a winged giantess Steropees the Lightning, and then with Bubble as leader they visit the Sun, penetrating to its heart, which, despite Woom-o-Rim's calling of the Sun ' heartless ' (p. 111), is found to be both beautiful and human (IX, 68; see *Morwyn,* I, 54). When Cad, who symbolises the cruder aspects of gianthood and hates the Sun, as did Uryen Quirm, arrives and starts to eat the Sun's heart, like Moloch eating the Moon in *Up and Out,* the action is so horrible that John o' Dreams kills him. The return to Dorset is made on a falling star, Lalanika.

Next, a Druid, who has the necessary magic for space-flight, takes John o' Dreams and Jilly to a star in the Milky Way called Vindex, where the Druids have founded a society dominating its strange people (XII, 88-9). They get Ring and Ting to join them and after various adventures among the strangely-formed inhabitants, they find the kindly Cerne Giant who lives there enslaved by another giant, the grim Bog, who has, like Myrddin Wyllt, vast ears, so that he hears everything that is uttered ' in every language in the multiverse ' (XVIII, 131-4; XXVI, 185). The Cerne Giant, sick of his slavery, kills the cruel Bog who is planning to eat our young people, and greets them kindlily. The Druid's flight-magic is possessed by two creatures, a worm and a slug, called Wug and Zug, who have grown to four feet high (XV, 115), and with their help they all take the Cerne Giant back to Dorset. The name ' Bog ' is symbolic.

Powys's many giants, to be grouped with other ancient powers, have hitherto, like those powers, been ethically ambiguous, but all symbolise strength and have a stature demanding respect. In both *Atlantis* and *The Mountains of the Moon* there were giants pleasant and unpleasant; and now a firm distinction is made between the ' wicked giant ' Cad and the ' good giant ' of Cerne Abbas (XXVIII, 200). The Cerne Giant has appeared in book after book. In *Wolf Solent* his ' phallic shamelessness ' was an item in Squire Urquhart's researches (XIV, 295 or 279; XVI, 332-3 or 316-7) and in the *Auto-biography* he is ' the great Phallic Giant ' (IV, 132). Dud No-man had his ' Cerne Giant ' stick. A chapter in *The Brazen Head* bore his name. In *Jobber Skald* and *The Brazen Head* he is a health-force. Now at last we meet him, and henceforward he dominates as a specifically *creative* agent.

Our problem of ' all or nothing ' converges on Space. Time is, as before, a poor rival, partly under our control (XVII, 129). But Space still teases Powys, to use Keats's phrase on eternity, ' out of thought '. Bubble insists that it is a Nothing destined to swallow all creation into an ' infinity ' of ' Nothingness ' (XI, 81-2). God, speaking through the Newt, after saying that He is the Universe and that ' empty space ' is his ' dwelling ', asks John o' Dreams to consider how matter and mind have come into existence out of Nothingness; and there is no solution, except that the old thought of ' another Dimension ' (XXI, 156-7), in *Up and Out* so strongly repudiated, recurs. Ring in medi-tation thinks that Space cannot be supposed to end anywhere; thinner than air, it is a nothing; and yet it is a nothing that is present and indeed everywhere; yet it has not any soul or mind; and the conclu-sion is that there is behind the whole problem ' a definite purpose ', showing ' us mortals ' our triviality (XXVIII, 198-9). Like John o' Dreams, he is forced to postulate *something else*.

We are down, nearly, to rock-bottom, or worse; space, Powys's final trust, is, at the limit, unthinkable. Our only help comes from the Cerne Giant. At the book's conclusion he communes with the Skull with whom, as a creative principle, he naturally gets on well (XXVIII,

206; XXX, 213). But before that we have our third adventure, devised by the creative Giant himself, and this is a voyage far into space beyond the stars to create a new star, so realising the book's recurring dream of filling space; that is, of creation. They take mould from Dorset as a start. On the way, John wonders if, were everything gone, would creation re-start on its own? It seems so, since their little new star quickly becomes quite a large one. Here they are visited by a new being : the Space-Monster.

It is a thing from Empty Space, amazingly formed. Its nature and habits are horrible. Though it is the only known creature in empty space, being nevertheless a creature, it comes up against the same insoluble problem. It cannot regard itself as 'the consciousness of Space'; there is still the 'gap' whereby its 'I' is not Space; subject and object are still separate. The Giant's answer, addressed rather widely to both Monster and the 'infinity of Space', is that Space cannot be finally separated as a thing-in-itself from what it contains; and it may contain *more than it knows*. Though they see only empty space, yet beyond all our knowledge there may be other masses of creation (XXVI, 182-8).

When the Space-Monster asks if Space is self-conscious and can say 'I am I', the Giant, always for the creative positives, replies 'that it most certainly has a self of its own' that can say 'I am I'; also that it is aware of its *limits;* but that then we face the great question, 'what lies behind' these limits? Here the Cerne Giant falls back on the authority of the great and all-hearing Bog, who had taught him that our sense-perception is aware of an aspect only, and that '*there are other Dimensions*', a 'parallel' world wherefrom all has a different aspect (XXVII, 190-2). We are back with the reading of man as 'amphibious' in *Mortal Strife*. But now we are to press further. Both Powys's scepticism and his strength derive from his existential and usually sex-centred allegiance. Such an allegiance forces us to suppose that man's 'amphibious' nature will react on and expand his sense-perception, including that of the sexual centres, which will not be answerable only to their biological function.

After our long story of Wordsworthian unions, cerebral lusts and obsessive fantasies, all in various ways unions of ego and opposite (pp. 58-9), and the teaching of a life-way of solitude and sensuality and 'diffused' (pp. 50, 59, 70) eroticism based on these, we ask, as we must ask of any ascetic philosophy, what of physiological functioning? Release may be had in sleep and dream, but that assumes a split personality, conscious from unconscious, and this Powys transcends (p. 46; *In Spite Of,* V, 128). Bog, 'who had ears for everything that went on in the whole universe' (XXVII, 192) and whose wisdom was accordingly *not limited to the demands of biological procreation on any one planet,* had given the Cerne Giant an answer:

> According to what Bog taught me, it would seem that life is much more complicated than in our childish minds we think it is. In the matter of sex, Bog taught me that what in the English language is called masturbation — that is to say, the excited emission of semen by the use of our imagination — is a much more important and creative act than ordinary and natural fornication or the raping, if we are male, of our feminine opposite.
>
> (XXVII, 192)

The activating power, we must note, is imaginative rather than physical. The teaching bears at least an indirect and analogic relation to Wolf's 'mythology' in *Wolf Solent,* which was called a 'spiritual vice' and given other relevant associations (XXIII, 568 or 541; and see pp. 33-4). It was also a battle of good-and-evil, ethically toned. Though a difference remains, moral conflict is present in both, since for the more physiological activity it seems that some element of evil, of the alien and daring, must be present as an activating agent; and to this experience even nature-unions, wherein the objectively alien is off-set against the ego, bear a certain relation. Mr Evans's making for himself sadistic dramas in *A Glastonbury Romance* and the cosmic 'orgasm of egocentric contemplation' there recorded (p. 39 above) are relevant; and the 'bosom houris' and 'stories' of the *Autobiography* (I, 8, 10; and see X, 537). How far in view of Powys's insistence on the infectious powers of thought (p. 59) the more dangerous fantasies may be indulged, remains unclear. Perhaps many may, as an expelling of psychological poisons; for it is true that mankind lives in a state of psychological constipation. In *The Art of Happiness* we are advised 'to lower our spiritual buckets' cautiously into what is 'bad' in order to cope with life's battles through use of a 'diffused sadism' (V, 203-4). A helpful statement occurs in *In Spite Of.* Whatever, he says, our insane perversities, Powys 'recommends, along with profound and absolute secrecy, a free indulgence for all the solitary ecstasies of the imagination' except only for 'the ecstasy of homicide'; this is a way to the unity of 'a new self-created self'; and though, as in nature-union, we through this 'indulgence' become temporarily one with the opposite of our self-engendered ' abortion ', we all the time know that what is ' permanently ourselves ' remains outside the good and the evil, and that we are merely ' playing at being saints and monsters '; that is, masochists and sadists (*In Spite Of*, V, 129-30, 137-8). In *Morwyn* the Golden Age was found *below* Hell.

What is counselled is a way of purification and integration, and has analogies throughout the narcissistic rhapsodies of *Thus Spake Zarathustra*.* It relates to the bases of poetic creation, the worst fantasy-stories and ' mythologies ' being nevertheless the raw and sexually-impregnated material for all excelling imaginations; it relates to the fall from Eden to the conflict-knowledge of good and evil basic to such activities, and to the use and transcending of this conflict-knowledge and our redemption into a new Golden Age. This is the power of ' unsatisfied desire ' in *A Glastonbury Romance* (IV, 112 or 126) and *Maiden Castle*, and the joy won from our ' secret selves ' in *Atlantis* (p. 97 above). It is the *Parthenogesis* of *The Brazen Head* defined by Ghosta : ' I am not losing my maidenhead, and yet I am drawing from the inmost depths of myself a dew-drop of living creation ' (XIV, 211). And yet it need not preclude normal sex-activity, but concerns rather that overplus in man that makes our civilisations and our insights beyond earth. The Cerne Giant, we are told, wants always to make love to some ' strange ' partner, and ' there is a " Cerne Giant " in every man ' (*The Art of Happiness*, III, 110).

Back in Dorset we have reminders, recalling *Jobber Skald*, of Portland Bill (XXVIII, 205-6). Our overall impressions are happy. Our questionings are accompanied by splendid descriptions of vast nature's fiery rondure and of ' something else ' in man equal to but different from the splendours, for which there are no words (V, 34-5; VI, 45). Rightly all is done as through the child-consciousness of a

---

* See my analyses in *Christ and Nietzsche* (1948) and *The Golden Labyrinth* (1962). I have discussed the relation of Nietzsche's doctrine to Powys's in *All or Nothing* in the Epilogue to the 1962 edition of *The Christian Renaissance*. The cathartic potentialities and *moral* implications of the sexual teaching delivered in *All or Nothing* had been emphatically stated in letters from Powys to myself dated 6, 18 and 23 January and 6 and 27 February, 1957. From these letters it appears that Powys did not succeed in mastering all his darker fantasies (p. 59 above), and was finally content not to have done so. The matter is not quite clear. Nor is it clear whether, or how far, physical assistance to the imaginative activity is allowed. From the letters it seems that for many people it might be, provided that the imagination is active too. For Powys's letters to me see p. 15 above.

nursery-tale, for to that innocence in us all the book's final doctrine is levelled. True, we shall not find Queen Boadicea, as do our young people, in the Tower of London, but that our book should end with this discovery chimes well with Powys's devotion to pre-Roman Britain.

On the great issue as to which will eventually win, ' eternal quiescence ' or ' everlasting activity ', it is within our own hearts — as we were told in *The Mountains of the Moon* (p. 112) — that the answer lies (XXXI, 219). So the majestic life-work draws to its close.

CHAPTER IX

Conclusion

I have been blazing trails in a virgin forest; it is pioneer work, and errors are likely. The ramifications are many and confusing. Shakespeare alone has left us literature of so vast and intricate a comprehension. The two developments are similar. Powys's poems, early narratives and lecturing correspond to Shakespeare's output before 1600; the famous sequence from *Wolf Solent* onwards to the dark tragedies; *Owen Glendower* and *Porius* to *Antony and Cleopatra* and *Coriolanus;* and both show final periods of myth and marvel, with a concentration on youth. Though Powys's technique is scarcely dramatic, his way of making each work a world of its own is Shakespearian, especially in his use of colourings: green for *Wolf Solent,* blue and purple for *A Glastonbury Romance,* white for *Jobber Skald,* red and gold for *Owen Glendower,* yellow for *Porius,* gold for *Atlantis.*

As always, certain strictures are possible. Powys can tire us by repetition; his vastly spatialised technique and massive deployments may intrude at the expense of narrative; and his mastery of the long sentence, like the wielding of a giant's club, tempts him, on occasion, too far. Nevertheless his choice of media has in the main been admirably attuned to his purposes. These are peculiarly his own; he is announcing a gospel, a *tao* or life-way, perhaps also a death-way, though when he likes, as in *The Meaning of Culture* (1930), he can write impersonally on a wide field.

To traditional religion he is deeply attuned while remaining sceptical. On Catholicism he comments with a peculiar sensitivity, especially in *The Meaning of Culture;* there and in both *The Pleasures of Literature* and *Mortal Strife* he writes profoundly of Christ; and for St Paul his admiration is consistent. Theological disquisition is wonderfully handled in *Owen Glendower* and *The Brazen Head.* For some of us the Christian and bisexual idealisms, for the two involve each other, of *Owen Glendower* will remain the summit of his achievement. However, he is impelled to speak for our disturbed and sceptical age, distrusting bisexual unities in *Porius* and *Atlantis* in association with theology and science, though bisexuality still *fascinates* in *The Mountains of the Moon* (140); rigid systems lead to tyranny and torture; all easy solutions he refuses, never forgetting the horrors in nature and in man. His own choicest precepts he admits to be provisional and he is aware, despite theology, that Chance, honoured in book after book, and perhaps especially in *The Inmates* (XV, 266; XVI, 309), is a determining power. But he also insists that from this ambiguous and indecipherable universe or multiverse, for he prefers the latter term, goodness, by which he means not zeal or ' love ' but rather tolerance, kindliness and humour, has somehow unaccountably arisen, to exert henceforward its own unavoidable compulsions (*Autobiography*, XII, 652; *A Glastonbury Romance*, XXVIII, 986 or 943). His gospel is not confined to generalities and probably his most important contribution to our religious tradition is his insistence that ' no religion that doesn't deal with sex-longing in some kind of way is much use to us ' (*Maiden Castle*, IX, 422).*

On science he is severe. He denies that the buying of knowledge by the cruelty of vivisection is justifiable and regards its worse excesses as criminal. Of reason he writes, in *Mortal Strife* :

> It is completely blocked in its approach to the reality of things by the obtruding presences of Time and Space, who like a pair of monstrous Punchinellos — one striking on the gong of a clock whose echoes refuse to cease, and the other emptying starry marbles out of a pocket that seems bottomless — so deafen and dazzle it that it takes electrons for living affections, mathematical symbols for living persons, and the extremely limited dimension that surrounds us for the Totality of Being.
>
> (VI, 95)

His own judgments, though based in part as they must be on past science, rely nevertheless as far as may be on common-sense, personal experience and sense-perception; though for him sense-perception is liable to be expanded by extra-sensory experience and imaginative power. His relation to modern poetry is at one point defined in a brilliantly modernistic fusillade :

> Their dominant note is a sardonic contempt for what they regard as the popular ' cliché ' in emotional reaction. Their desire to be

---

* When I last visited Powys (on 27 January, 1963) he spoke hardly at all, but pointed vigorously to a sexual symbol, and knotted tight one finger in the other hand, using sign-language.

original is feverish and frantic; and taking the short cut to their fulfilment they become obscure. They set themselves to deal out pain instead of pleasure, and riddles in place of revelation. They make mock at idealism with the puritanical zest of religious zealots. They force themselves to face up to their awareness of their lack of real imagination by an awareness of this awareness as a higher poetic dimension. In their loathing for the obvious they become idiotic. In their contempt for the commonplace they nourish abortions. In their hatred for daylight they veer between the kaleidoscopical and the pyrotechnical. Under the spell of their weakness and their melancholy the poor captive Muse is forced to dance on a wire in bangles and spangles, while she exchanges conundrums not only with the weary clown in the arena, but with excited clergymen in the audience.

(Obstinate Cymric, VIII, 121)

Here Powys for once measures himself against his adversaries in their own, sharp, terms.

He announces the possibility of a greater consciousness for man, embracing phenomena with *all* the senses simultaneously; faculties of smell — his books are loaded with olfactory impressions — of eating, and of sex are to join with sight and hearing to create a new totality of response, unconstricted by the use of separate sense-inlets in isolation. This wholeness has its own limitations. In sexual matters he concentrates more on cerebral lusts than on physical unions, and in the *Autobiography* writes boldly that he is ' not one for the normal rites of love ', while remaining totally ' unashamed of this peculiarity ' (X, 537). His recurring emphasis on cold-blooded life-forms specifically supports his doctrine of an ' etherealised ', ' diffused ' and conscious sensuality pointing to ' the evolution of a higher race ' in line with the golden age of Cronos (*Morwyn*, I, 53-4; III, 219-20; and see *Maiden Castle*, IX, 473; *Owen Glendower*, VII, 250).* There is a difference from the teaching of D. H. Lawrence. Whatever our views, the insistence is on an honouring of sexual instinct, even, at the limit, of normal instinct, as may be seen from Porius' sexual adventure with the giantess. There are many attendant complications; as things are, the fully integrated, or near-integrated, man must of necessity be, in a sense, bisexual (*In Spite Of*, VII, 222; and see p. 61). That is why there is so great an emphasis on bisexuality

---

* Those interested in Powys's relation of certain aspects of his sex-gospel to Thibet (p. 45 above; and see Index C, ' Thibetan Wisdom ') might care to consult Garma C. C. Chang's — rather abstruse — *Teachings of Tibetan Yoga* (University Books, New York, 1963).

in the narratives, though passing criticisms, as in the early *Rodmoor* and the late *Atlantis,* may on occasion be strong. In both *The Art of Happiness* and *The Art of Growing Old* Powys writes with uncanny insight on the *psychic* relationship of man and woman. He is simultaneously aware of the demands of sexual difference and of the authority of the bisexual intuition; the state of being in love *is* the bisexual state (*The Art of Happiness,* III, 100-3; IV, 179). Powys can regard the deepest self both as differentiated and as bisexual (*In Spite Of,* V, 128; VII, 222). Male youth, corresponding to what I designate the 'seraphic intuition', remains, from first to last, a star.

The health radiating from Powys's books flowers from an acceptance of the baffling co-presence in the human psyche of sexually prompted delight with what is simultaneously repudiated by ethic.

On our last, specifically creative, quest in *All or Nothing* our leader is the great and good Cerne Giant, slayer of Bog and now freed from slavery. Bog lived like Oom (p. 110 above) in the bowels of his world, the star Vindex, and was himself made in part of rock. Now these deep and craggy under-powers, so long in Powys authoritative, give place to more etheric quests. Similarly, the Cerne Giant, symbol of sex-prompted and therefore sadistic violence, is, in attunement to the Nietzschean gospel — 'Now is that become thy final refuge which hath been hitherto thine extremest peril' (*Thus Spake Zarathustra,* 45) — our final guide towards a new creation. But the dark forces have been necessary. Was not the Grail messenger (pp. 39-40) called 'hideous'? And though the all-knowing Bog, whose very name suggests gross powers which Powys has elsewhere (p. 85 above) related to the Grail, has been justly slain, his deep counsel remains, handed on by his slayer. That counsel, which we have already (pp. 119-20) discussed, sinks deep; more, it is explosive. Pope, Blake, Nietzsche and Lawrence all asserted the primacy of instinct, and Keats in his letter-journal to George and Georgiana Keats (14 February–3 May, 1819; especially 19 March and 15 April; Letters, ed. B. F. Forman, 316-17, 336-7), a letter of strong relevance to our argument, urged a *provisional* acceptance of dangerous energies and passions. Powys goes farther. He *says* what they probably all *meant.* For we are here at the very heart of the long reiterated marriage of good and evil, Taliessin's 'mystical light' coming 'from the most noisome regions of evil' in *Morwyn* (p. 66 above), a mystery so often in literature stated but left undefined and inconclusive. Powys is precise: he meets Lawrence's recognition, stated at the conclusion to 'The Real Thing', that regeneration 'is not a question of knowing something but of doing something' (*Phoenix*, 1936; p. 203; and see 'The Reality of Peace'). How much good counsel of apparent profundity is in effect no more than a mental influence? But Powys works on the one pivot of man's earthly, psychic-physical, being. The 'doing' advocated, which Lawrence too, urging acceptance of the 'sickening' thing within, the 'serpent of secret and shameful desire' in the psyche, all but stated in 'The Reality of Peace' (*Phoenix*, 675-80), is the free and waking use of the giant enginry of sex-located instinct, *whatever the nature of its fantasies, which vary with each of us*, for what is, in effect, a creative end.

Though the Cerne Giant is a comprehensive symbol who presides equally over an ordinary sexual encounter in *The Brazen Head*, that needs no advertisement. It is his more esoteric teaching, learned from Bog, that most needs our attention, since it places and uses that over-plus of sexual sap that percolates throughout man's being, and prompts his more than biological advance. Like animals, instincts can best be tamed by those who make friends with them, with their own wild selves. The Giant's teaching points the way to imaginative and physical self-enjoyment, self-knowledge, and therefore, inevitably, self-criticism; to freedom nevertheless from the ethical prison-self and ever new liberty within the re-created self; to recognition of God's mysteriously implanted design;* to humility and integrity and trust; and all without harm or hurting to another. This may be the very 'soul-making' that Keats was labouring to define. It is the mind's most intimate, electric, union with that physical nature with which it finds itself entwined, and may indeed be the basis of all Wordsworthian insights, Wolf Solent's 'mythology' being the link (pp. 33-5, 119-20). On every level there is, as we have already (pp. 58-9) argued, a union of ego and opposite, psychic or material. This 'opposite' will be, or seem, dark and female (pp. 60-1) as opposed to daylight reason; Dionysian against Apollonian. The union prompts and conditions, as union with the instincts of a bludgeoning giant prompted and conditioned the

---

* The religious term 'God' is mine. Perhaps the counsel in question, as on a similar occasion I suggested in my preface to *Christ and Nietzsche*, assumes prayer or at least a *prayerful state*, ingrained from childhood: both Nietzsche and Powys were the sons of clergymen. See too my discussion of 'the God within the mind' in Pope's *Essay on Man*, as developed in *Laureate of Peace*, V, 178; also my analysis of the *Essay*, II, 43-56.

sweet and saving wisdom of Powys's books, the noblest artistic creation.* Physical power becomes spiritual power. Worst evil becomes
highest good. In the solitary sex-life lies the golden key.

Within the workshop of lonely self-conflict and gradual integration
there are many complexities and many dark smithies, as Nietzsche's
Thus Spake Zarathustra so excellently records, and intellectual
formulations are difficult. In Powys's writings ' evil ' terms may, as
in Blake's also, be misleading. Powys's thinking uses, but is not
controlled by, ethic; it is his consistent practice to present many of his
more interesting and meaningful persons with repellent exteriors
and to describe them by denigratory phrases. What he is doing is to
push through, without reserve or cant, the darkest substances — a good
example occurs in *The Art of Happiness* (V, 203) — searching always
for a greater good. ' Greater ', for the purpose involves a new stature
for man, and new powers; and these are often symbolised by the
traditional medium of giants, or men of massive build. As in our
enjoyment of ancient epics, physical strength may be an objective
corrclative to our sense of psychic powers; if it were not so our
enjoyment of their fisticuffs would be an adolescent reversion. In
Homer and the Aether (Preface, 10) Powys tells us that Homer will
not be readily outdated since his fights may be allowed to correspond
to whatever mental, or magical, fights in which futurity may involve
mankind; battles, that is, of mind-control and mesmerism, using
powers such as those of Morsimmon Esty in *The Inmates* and Peter
Peregrinus in *The Brazen Head*.

That Powys himself has exerted thaumaturgic powers is clear from
the *Autobiography*. For him human beings are not the only, or even
the most important, objects of amatory approach : the external
universe itself is more *basic,* being ' the natural bride and natural
bridegroom of every creature's soul ' (*In Spite Of,* IV, 116). This
Wordsworthian union Powys extends to a sense of soul, or astral,
projection, the partly liberated astral body being attached to the

---

* In a letter on my *Times Literary Supplement* article of 11 October, 1957,
Powys wrote: ' Nobody but you has brought into an analysis of me as a writer
the one essential thing — namely that I was born a sadist.' Powys's life-work
represents an acceptance and transmutation of a dangerous instinct which is
simultaneously that life-work's central thrust and activation. For those who
accept the commentaries on the poem offered in *Christ and Nietzsche* (IV, 136)
and *The Starlit Dome* (IV, 301-4), the process may be regarded as poetically
defined in Keats' *Ode to Psyche*.

physical by a gleaming or silver cord (pp. 83, 88). Owen Glendower, as we have seen, could even appear to others at a distance. So, if we accept a report by Theodore Dreiser, could Powys himself. I quote from W. E. Woodward's *The Gift of Life* (III, 65):*

Dreiser said that when he was living in New York, on West Fifty-seventh Street, John Cowper Powys came occasionally to dinner. At that time Powys was living in this country, in a little town about thirty miles up the Hudson, and he usually left Dreiser's place fairly early to catch a train to take him home. One evening, after a rather long after-dinner conversation, Powys looked at his watch and said hurriedly that he had no idea it was so late, and he would have to go at once or miss his train. Dreiser helped him on with his overcoat and Powys, on his way to the door, said, ' I'll appear before you, right here, later this evening. You'll see me '.

' Are you going to turn yourself into a ghost, or have you a key to the door?' Dreiser laughed when he asked that question, for he did not believe for an instant that Powys meant to be taken seriously.

' I don't know yet,' said Powys, ' I may return as a spirit or in some other astral form '.

Dreiser said that there had been no discussion whatever, during the evening, of spirits, ghosts, or visions. The talk had been mainly about American publishers and their methods. He said that he gave no further thought to Powys's promise to reappear, but he sat up reading for about two hours, all alone. Then he looked up from his book and saw Powys standing in the doorway between the entrance hall and the living room. The apparition had Powys's features, his tall stature, loose tweed garments and general appearance, but a pale white glow shone from the figure. Dreiser rose at once, and strode towards the ghost, or whatever it was, saying, ' Well, you've kept your word, John. You're here. Come on in and tell me how you did it '. The apparition did not reply, and it vanished when Dreiser was within three feet of it.

As soon as he had recovered somewhat from his astonishment Dreiser picked up the telephone and called John Cowper Powys's house in the country. Powys came to the phone, and Dreiser recognised his voice. After he had heard the story of the apparition Powys said, ' I told you I'd be there, and you oughtn't to be surprised '. Dreiser told me that he was never able to get any explanation from Powys, who refused to discuss the matter from any standpoint.

---

* A work of personal reminiscences by the biographer of Washington, Lafayette, Tom Paine and Evelyn Prentice. *The Gift of Life* was published in 1947 by E. P. Dutton & Co, Inc, New York, to whom I express my gratitude for granting me permission to quote this extract.

If Powys had indeed any such power it is reasonable that it should have been exercised in psychic collaboration with the magnetic Dreiser whom he regarded as, after Thomas Hardy, 'the most arresting human being I have ever met' (*The Art of Growing Old,* VI, 93).*

But these unions and soul-projections are themselves only half the story. In Powys's later development time, so long a prepossession at least in so far as power was felt calling from a distant past, loses prestige, while space becomes an obsession; and yet, even so, space cannot satisfy, nor can it be coherently thought of for long; it is only the *one side* of reality and at the last, after various attempts at scepticism, another dimension has, as so often before, to be posited.

Though Powys's writings are saturated in occultism, and though he maintains a firm sense of thought as power and also as existing not in, but around, the physical, within ' some magnetic causal dimension for which at present we have no name ' (*Jobber Skald,* XII, 451, 453), yet he is as often sceptical as expectant of human survival, a problem to which he returns in book after book. What he labours for is some replacing of Wordsworth's ' pleasure that there is in life itself ' by a pleasure covering both life *and* death (*The Art of Happiness,* I, 42-4, 47); but whether that ' pleasure ' involves survival is not settled. His latest statement occurs in the preface to the 1961 reissue of *Wolf Solent,* where he asserts that, ' whatever death may mean, and none of us really know ', he expects and desires no continuance for himself. The more creative expositions of *The Mountains of the Moon* and *All or Nothing* open wider possibilities; and he has warned us to rate such ' cubic ' works in the artistic dimension as the more authoritative (p. 62). Despite his occult affinities and his application of the term ' medium ' to himself (*Letters to Louis Wilkinson,* 8 Jan., 1952; 284), the evidence of Spiritualism is not discussed.†

---

* The only other great writer of whom I have heard anything similar is Lord Byron, who was reported, though by whom I cannot recall, as having been met in London when he was known to be at Missolonghi. On this difficult subject a mass of material has been assembled by Robert Crookall in *The Study and Practice of Astral Projection;* London, 1961. See also Andrija Puharich's *The Sacred Mushroom;* London, 1959.

† That Powys did have séance experience of spirit communication is clear from an incident described in Maurice Browne's *Too Late to Lament* (London, 1955; XII, 205), and discussed further by Mr Glyn Hughes in *Two Worlds* (No. 3842; March, 1964). That since dying Powys has had experience of earth-communication has been witnessed by a message through Miss Frances Horsfield recorded in *Psychic News* (No. 1625; 27 July, 1963).

Powys follows the instinct of a true poet to keep as close as he can to his own sensory and extra-sensory perceptions. He is happier using a talking skull than a disembodied spirit (pp. 107, 115). His telepathic (pp. 101, 113) clubs and ' psychic ' (*Autobiography*, XII, 644) sticks function as spirit-guides. The Cerne Giant is a Powysian guide, and so Powys, like Dud No-man (p. 50), carried a heavy ' Cerne Giant ' stick: a picture of him holding it appears in Louis Marlow's (i.e. Louis Wickinson's) *Welsh Ambassadors* (facing p. 24). The comparatively idyllic tone of *Jobbler Skald* is marked by Sylvanus Cobbold's carrying of a light soldier'e cane. Powys's concrete symbolisms are very exactly devised. His aim is to work from, speak through and induce, not knowledge but sensation and experience; and further to announce the possibility of a new, creative, step in evolution awaiting man (p. 88; and see p. 19). Working from close contact with the sex-drive he apprehends magical powers already housed in man but awaiting development, of which his giants and cumbrous magi are rough symbols.

He may, despite his elemental and occult inclusions, be called a great humanist. Man he sees as a miracle, as Blake saw his ' Tyger ', and if any one passage were to be chosen to sum up his message it might be this, from *The Meaning of Culture* :

Deep should be our philosophic awareness of the extraordinary drama in which we are all involved; this life of which not one day is a replica of the last, these encounters whose crucial and terrible importance may never be recognised, or only recognised long afterwards when it is all too late. It is a monstrous thing, the way we all drift and jostle and barge against one another without any method or any awareness of what is going on between us. Skeletons, clothed in flesh, clothed in coverings stolen from other animals, we talk, jest, and scold. But the look from the eyes of a living being is a strange and terrible look, not easy to be discounted. What is it that gazes forth, so grim, so furtive, from the eye of a man? None knoweth! There may be yet some deep, undiscovered power in human personality that will one day crack the complacent walls of this tough world and plant the crazy gonfalon of its impious importunity in some plane of existence altogether beyond the mathematical fourth dimension. Meanwhile, involved as we all are in the same tragic imbroglio, our feelings, our minds, our nerves all vibrating to old totems and old taboos, encrusted with old, dark, perilous superstitions, nourished by old, deep, bitter-sweet earth-wisdom, it is an impertinence for any among us to separate ourselves from the rest and patronise the rest.

(XI, 288)

The passage includes much of Powys, but not all.

For there is no humour in it; and no student of Powys will get far who does not respond to the pervasive humour saturating his writings and often colouring with cunning irony his most abysmal speculations. And with this goes a wonderful courtesy, unusual in our day, not only to his readers but also to his own fictional persons whose rights, as persons, are never invaded, never scorned, never forgotten.

I have used the word ' abysmal ' : for we have followed Powys in his downward quest below Earth, below Hell, in search through evil and what Shakespeare called ' the dark backward and abysm of time ' for the lost golden age; and then, present space overruling past time, we have adventured to the furthest limits of space on a more etheric quest, the Sun or the divine Aether replacing the Saturnian gold.

If one were to figure out a visual symbol of Powys's total accomplishment, it would be, I suppose, a Cerne Giant, backed by granite, body swathed in mists and cudgel resting on Earth; an expression combining the tormented thought of Dostoievsky and the laughter of Rabelais; eyes raised from Sea to Aether, head gilded by the Sun.

Postscript

For an important correspondence in the teaching of a famous oriental seer to the counsel discussed on pp. 119-20 and 125-7 above, see C. B. Purdom, *The God-Man;* London, 1964; on page 286.

INDEXES

*References in Footnotes are Indexed simply under the number
of the page on which the notes
occur*

A. WORKS OF JOHN COWPER POWYS

133

B. PERSONS; PUBLISHERS; PERIODICALS

C. IMAGINATIVE POWERS